Contents

Introduction 9

Chapter 1: Ideas that Sell: Bringing Your Product to Life 13

  Starting the Process: Coming Up with an Idea That Sells 16

    Brainstorming 18

    Flexibility 19

    Critical Thinking 20

    Don't Forget the Small Stuff 21

    Positivity Over Everything 22

  What Do YOU Think? 22

    Expand on What You Already Know 25

    Observe Quietly, Then Challenge 26

    Market Research 28

  Creating Your First Product to Test 31

  Defining Data Types 34

  When to Revise Your Product 35

    Disparity 36

    Pricing 36

    Poor Packaging 38

    Similarities 39

  Tips for Bringing Your Idea to Life: Creating the Prototype 40

    Coherency and Minimalism 40

Restricting Your Creativity to Spark Better Ideas 41

It Doesn't Have to be Perfect 42

Learn and Practice the 4 P's of Marketing 42

Product/Service 44

Place 45

Price 46

Promotion 46

Chapter 2: Prototypes and Product Testing 48

Why Prototype? 50

To Test and Refine 50

Test Materials 51

Literal Description 52

Shows Earnestness 52

Planning a Prototype 53

Concept Sketch 53

Digital Sketch 54

Building a Prototype 55

Using a 3-D Printer 56

Deconstruct the Competition 57

Don't Aim for Perfection 58

Testing Your Prototype: Taking the Next Step 59

Soliciting Feedback 60

Testing Your Invention with the Right People 62

Be an Unbiased Party and Adapt Willingly 64

Gather Feedback and Keep Trying 66

What Comes Next? 66

Chapter 3: Patents and Manufacturing *68*

Patents 71

Provisional Patent Applications 73

Trade Secrets Law 75

Trademarks 78

Shape 78

Building Design 79

Ornamental Color or Design 79

Phrases 79

Symbols 80

Copyrights 82

Trade Dress Unfair Competition Laws 84

Guidelines for Additional Protection 87

Do your research 88

Non-Disclosure Agreement (NDA) 89

Non-Compete Agreement 90

Work for Hire Agreement 90

Manufacturing Your Product 91

To Outsource or Not to Outsource? 92

Finding a Factory 94

What to Look for in a Factory 96

Knowing What Questions to Ask 98

Finding Investors for Your Invention 99

Finding Angel Investors 100

Tips for Securing Funding 102

Put the Fun in Crowdfunding 102

Gain a Reputation 103

Utilize Accelerators 104

Chapter 4: Building Brands & Following Trends 105

What is a brand? 106

The 7 Steps of Establishing a Brand Identity 109

1. Research 109

2. Choose your focus 110

3. Choose a name 111

4. Choose a catchphrase. 114

5. Choose your colors and fonts. 116

6. Design your logo. 119

7. Apply, evolve, and grow. 124

Marketing Your Product 126

Product Marketing vs. Conventional Marketing 129

Competitive Pricing vs. Value-Based Product Pricing 130

4 Tips for Successful Marketing 132

Digital Marketing 137

From Idea to Launch

Take your Great Idea to Profitable Reality

Sell your New Invention, Innovation, Brand, Product, Service & Business Ideas: Think it, Make it, Launch it, Sell it & Profit from it!

By

Nathan McKenzie

Copyrighted Material

Copyright © 2020 – *CSBA Publishing House*

Email:csbapublishing@gmail.com

All Rights Reserved.

No part of this publication may be reproduced, stored in a retrieval system or transmitted in any form or by any means, electronic, mechanical, photocopying, recording or otherwise without the proper written consent of the copyright holder, except brief quotations used in a review.

Published by:

CSBA Publishing House

Cover & Interior designed

By

Robin Hurst

First Edition

Digital Marketing Basics 138

How Does Internet Marketing Work? 139

Digital Marketing Strategy Guide **142**

Utilizing Smartphones 142

Social Media Advertising 144

Facebook Ads 144

Instagram Ads 149

Google Ads 153

4 Specific Tips for Getting the Most Out of Social Media Advertising **155**

1. Set a Budget 155

2. Practice Relevancy 156

3. Invest in the Visuals 157

4. Create Strong Landing Pages 157

Chapter 5: Ready to Launch *159*

Internal v. External: Launching Your Product **160**

Internal Product Launch 161

5 Ways to Hold a Successful External Product Launch 165

Managing Your Inventory **172**

Calibrate your forecasting 173

Use the FIFO strategy (first in, first out). 173

Keep a close eye on the units that sell, and the ones that don't. 174

Set up a system to routinely audit your inventory. 175

Think about investing in inventory management software. 175

Manage your assets as they wear down. 176

Never sacrifice quality. 176

Dropshipping could be the key. 177

Knowing When It's Time to Expand 178

You have more business than your team can handle. 178

You have a strong team that you can trust. 179

You are running out of space. 181

You are meeting your goals. 181

You have the funds to make it happen. 182

Selling Your Invention and Taking a Payoff 182

How to Sell Your Idea to a Company 183

Taking a Payoff 184

Taking a Percentage of Sales 185

Do You Want to Give the Idea Away? 186

Conclusion *188*

Introduction

"Inventing is a combination of brains and materials. The more brains you use, the less material you need." -Charles Kettering

I came across my own invention by accident. I didn't spend years dreaming up dozens of devices or drawing the plans for life-altering technology. But, it did start with an idea. A small, simple one that I believed could work if done right and done well. I was never the smartest kid in school, and I didn't major in business or engineering or product development in college. To be honest, my life up until my invention had been just average. But that didn't stop me from trying, from giving everything I had to make my idea come to life.

Thank you for taking the time to download my book. I know there are dozens of manuscripts out there that probably have good and useful information. So, it means a great deal to me that you trust my knowledge and experience to help you in your journey of bringing your idea to launch.

I wrote this book hoping to influence someone just like me, a regular person who wants to create something and show them the possibilities that come with being an innovator. To share my own personal insights from having started my product in my kitchen and bringing it to market, and finding unbelievable success that I only ever dreamed of.

So, once again, thank you for allowing me to be a part of your adventure.

This book begins right where it should -at the creation. Even the best authors get writer's block, and the best inventors lose their muse, so I thought it only appropriate to start at the beginning of an idea. I will teach you how to stimulate creativity, brainstorm ideas, and finally locate a sustainable and realistic product that will become your invention. Then, we move onto what it takes to bring that idea to life, crafting prototypes, locating manufacturers, enlisting the help of carpenters, tech developers, and anyone who can assist in creating the physical adaption of your idea.

I wanted to not only help you think of something that you can create, but also push you to create it, and then sell it. After all, we innovators only create so that others can utilize our creations, right? This is why I dedicated a great portion of this book to also help you sell your idea. I've included the most in-depth research for social media marketing, brand development, package designing, and so much more to help you deliver the total package.

During my time as an inventor, I have come across too many innovators who have sat on an idea, waiting for the right time to start. Inventors who did their best to share their products with the world, only to miss the mark in their marketing strategies and fail. Creators who lost the rights to their work because they didn't know how to secure legal protection. In this book, you will find the answers to all of your questions. It is the complete roadmap that will undoubtedly guide your product to success.

This book will teach you absolutely everything you need to know about creating prototypes, building a brand around your product, protecting your intellectual property and plans, selling your idea for a profit, and so much more. I have no doubt in my mind that if you follow the advice detailed within these pages that you will see your idea through all the way to launch.

So, grab a notebook and a pen because we have a lot of work to do.

Let's get started!

Chapter 1: Ideas that Sell: Bringing Your Product to Life

Every time you turn on the computer, tune into the T.V., or open up an app on your smartphone, the screen is lit up by colorful advertisements that span from ingenious to purely entertaining. Products that you could have never dreamed of, apps that seem to do it all, even books from new authors are at the centerfold of your daily scrolling and general web browsing. It seems like just about everyone has an idea for the latest greatest contribution to the fast-moving modern world. And out of all these funny, smart, and current ideas, you can't help but think I can think of something even better (or maybe you already have).

If you are the creative type, you know firsthand that the wheels of invention never stop turning and that right now, you can name at least five ideas or products out of thin air. Coming up with a great idea isn't necessarily a problem, having a plan of action or even just some sort of guidance is what's stopping you from pursuing even just one invention. Or you may be an engineer by nature. You know how to execute a plan and are good with your mind and your hands, but can't come up with a viable idea or product if someone paid you a million dollars.

I'm here to show you that regardless of whether or not you have a notebook filled with names for potential products, or you just want to learn about what makes an idea great, you can take a thought, a concept, and turn it into a successful and potentially life-altering reality for millions of people. I know because I've done it.

I started my business in my kitchen, after realizing that something was missing in my own morning routine. I figured that if the right person had the right idea and formula to make it work, my problem would be solved, and that person would be a millionaire. And then I realized that I can be that person. My idea centered around the concept of a personalized bath product. I spent a year just doing research and experimenting until I finally found a way to make my dream a real-life miracle. It definitely wasn't easy, and at times I got so frustrated I couldn't even look at my work for weeks.

But after three years of testing, trying, and failing over and over again, learning how to create and run a business, and finally expanding out of my own home and hiring staff, I was able to sell my business for a profit. Unfortunately, for the time being, my NDA (non-disclosure agreement) keeps me from saying too much about the specifics of the product I created.

But in the end, I never thought that the whole crazy journey would happen, and the lessons I learned along the way are truly invaluable. This is why I decided to write this book with the premise of "Idea to Launch." I knew that there were a lot of others out there who were just like me who were looking for a way to make their ideas a reality or even just wanting to learn what it takes to go from punching the nine-to-five clock to working on a passion project full-time. And if I can help one person bring their idea to life, then I know that I did my part in helping the entrepreneur community.

I do have to warn you to prepare yourself. There is a reason that only a handful of ideas succeed in the business world. It isn't just about business; this is almost one hundred percent classified as self-development. You will be challenged in new ways that can encourage you to grow into a better, more determined, and more disciplined version of yourself. If you're ready and willing to approach this process with an open mind and let curiosity drive your intuition, then this will be a fun and fulfilling journey.

Starting the Process: Coming Up with an Idea That Sells

It is difficult to determine whether great ideas foster creative and unique trends, or if popular ideas from the outside world spark invention. Regardless of where the circle of invention truly begins, the undeniable truth is that applied observation, critical thinking, and thoughtfulness are necessary if you want to invent something. With observation and deep thought comes the need for an open mind, to come up with new ideas and take a good idea and make it great.

The world as we know it today has been shaped solely by progressive inventions and innovators who pushed and expanded the boundaries of technology, commerce, art, and nearly every other area of human interest that you can think of. The world's history has been written and determined by the mere pursuit of invention. Regardless of the inventor's underlying motive, there is no denying that ideas and actionable pursuit are the secret ingredients to creation.

Unfortunately, there is no exact manual that I can show you that will tell you how to take an idea and turn it into a million dollars overnight. What I can do is take everything I know from my many years of experience and applied knowledge, and the extensive history of invention and praised innovators, and catalyze the creative and practical processes.

In thinking of an invention, the starting point is knowing what questions to ask oneself. What problems are you personally facing, and in follow up: what solution can you think of that would solve just one of those problems. That is the fundamental key to a successful product. Most new ideas on the market attempt to solve a problem. If you have a cold, you take cold medicine.

If your shampoo isn't working as well as you want, there are personalized soaps that give you what you need. From "to-do list" apps to lights that turn on at the sound of a clap, there isn't a limit on how creative or different your ideas can be. Once you have identified a problem, you will know what you want to invent to create a solution for it. I know it's hard to think of something on the spot, so don't feel pressured at this very moment. However, here are a few tips that will help get your creative wheels turning.

Brainstorming

This may sound like an obvious trick, but sometimes it helps to put all of your ideas on paper and let your mind wander through the possibilities. Think about your areas of expertise, what are your hobbies, where do you work, and so on. Identify a problem (even just a small one that doesn't seem like a big deal), and jot down any notes, ideas, and questions that come to your head. Take just ten or fifteen minutes, and then go back through each idea and examine the possibilities.

Flexibility

I hate to break it to you, but a lot of times, the first idea that comes to you isn't always the best. There's nothing wrong with evaluating and restructuring your ideas to make them better. Think of the process that came with writing an essay for school.

The teacher made you brainstorm, write the first draft, revise, and write as many drafts as it took to get a final, perfect copy.

Revisiting your idea, with all the possibilities and factors that come with solving a problem, will help you to look at the problem and solution from different angles and see it from every perspective possible. As an innovator, you want to know your product inside and out.

Critical Thinking

I know from experience that this one can be confusing and even difficult for many aspiring inventors. We spend most of our childhood and early adulthood in school, learning to adopt a very narrow black-or-white mindset. But we all know that the world doesn't work that way, not everything is black or white. There are many grey areas, which leaves room for creativity and flexibility. When it comes to coming up with a good idea or fine-tuning a product, critical thinking is what will save your invention.

Thinking critically requires you to compare and contrast any existing solutions that will be challenging your product's purpose. It can also help you see any cracks that are already forming within your idea. Perhaps the solution to the problem you're trying to fix is actually caused by something you never thought of before? With a common cold, there are several symptoms that accompany it, coughing, sneezing, fatigue.

Many people opt for treating the symptoms, rather than the actual problem: the virus. You don't want your solution to be a bandage that diverts the attention away from the true problem, easing the symptoms, but not actually helping solve the issue. Think critically, and you will have strengthened your idea or even realized that you were too focused on a much smaller, less important symptom.

Don't Forget the Small Stuff

While it would be nice if everyone could think of a solution that creates world peace and ends world hunger, it isn't a realistic approach to coming up with ideas.

Most people want to make a large, positive impact, and that's great! But the small stuff is also important. Inventing a robot that will do your housework and walk the dog sounds like an amazing idea, but can you actually put it into practice and develop a business plan to match? Most likely, the answer is 'no.' And that's okay!

There are a thousand small problems or undiscovered uses for everyday items that directly impact our lives on the day-to-day. Spend about ten minutes thinking up different and practical uses for common objects.

This will help you practice creative and quick thinking within a limited time frame while focusing on the smaller details of a problem.

Positivity Over Everything

Like I said before, this game of invention and product launch is not for everybody. It's even more of a challenge mentally than it is physically.

Sometimes it will seem like there just isn't a solution to a problem, or that you're just one person trying to make a big difference.

But remember that winning comes with many failures. Don't be discouraged if a product idea doesn't stick, or that your solution doesn't pan out the way you thought it would.

Even Thomas Edison had hundreds of ideas that were unfulfilled at the time of his death. Enjoy the process and let your imagination run free.

What Do YOU Think?

I've had some really bad days in the last few years. I've been late to work because the bus didn't come on time, I dropped my phone in water, and all the personal content in it was destroyed, and just another dozen or so little things that we all as humans have faced.

On the surface, these small everyday happenings may sound trivial and easy to live with, because they don't happen often. But sometimes you go through a span of time when one bad thing after another seems to happen to you. While any other day, you would normally shrug it off and say, "oh well, life happens!" Today, I want you to focus for just a moment on the negativity.

Let me explain. Before the process of creating something new, Canadian entrepreneur Miki Agrawal asks herself, "what sucks in my world?" This simple, yet personal question has led Agrawal to run several socially conscious businesses, and create a global sanitation monopoly. When it comes to finding motivation in pursuing an idea or product, she says that every product she sells is helping someone who is in desperate need or that it is helping solve a global crisis.

Exercise 1: I want you to do an exercise right now. Grab a piece of paper and a pen, or just use the memos app on your phone, and write down five problems that you face on a regular or semi-regular basis. Not necessarily huge and critical issues, but just general dilemmas that are identifiable on a universal level.

Expand on What You Already Know

Awesome, you've written down your first five problems. Just like that, the first step to finding the next great idea, or at least a pretty good one, is already done. We'll come back to those five later. For now, let's talk more about brainstorming and creativity. One of the secrets to creating a great product is by expanding on a solution that already exists. In my opinion, too many aspiring entrepreneurs want to create something awesome but are too focused on coming up with something new and fresh. Obviously, you can't and should never steal someone else's invention or concept. But, you do have the option of expanding on a product that already exists.

Many creative people build off of others who came before them and then develop and evolve that creation into something even greater or all-encompassing. Take, for instance, the case of Renaissance mathematician Luca Pacioli, one of the most famous accountants in history. He popularized the double-entry system, which was thought of hundreds of years before he was born.

Even though Pacioli didn't invent the double-entry system, he brought it greater recognition and use so that people still use it even today. Don't get the wrong impression, he didn't just use this method all the time and tell people how great it was.

He wrote an entire treatise on mathematics in 1494, and twenty-seven pages of that book were just about the concept of double-entry bookkeeping. He dedicated time and effort to enforce the importance of this invention when it came to operating a business.

Pacioli's story goes to show that you don't have to be super creative or even a genius to discover something that makes an impact on the world. A great invention can stem from any number of inspirations and leads. Which brings me to your next exercise.

Exercise 2: Write down five already existing products or ideas that can be improved upon.

Observe Quietly, Then Challenge

Believe it or not, you can teach yourself how to be more creative. The fundamental basis for creativity comes from challenging what is given to you and then offering other solutions regardless of practicality. Having a creative mindset allows you to gain new perspectives on ordinary things around you. The ability to remain still and simply observe is not commonly practiced in our fast-paced, ever-changing modern world.

Everyone is rushing to do something, be somewhere, and live a lifestyle that is envied by others. But very few people stop their hectic schedules to be still and ponder all the things around them. Observational skills help you to learn, recall, and deepen your mindset within your immediate environment. This is crucial when coming up with new inventions and ideas.

Think of this upcoming exercise as a break from the encompassing box that is your mind. As part of a society that is constantly stimulated by technology, we habitually tend to overthink things. We get trapped within our own minds, creating endless loops of questioning the same things and never truly making creative advancements.

By either putting yourself into a completely new environment or disassociating with the one you're currently in, you allow your mind to slow down and take in its surroundings in a new and creative way. This can also be applied to solving the problem that you've identified. Sometimes we go for an over-complicated answer when a much simpler and obvious one is in front of you the whole time.

Exercise 3: Go out to a new place (or change the room you are in if you can't leave your home), and quietly sit and observe your surroundings. Take twenty minutes to notice things you've never seen before, feel how the environment affects your mood or thoughts, and listen to the sounds or stillness that surrounds you. After the twenty minutes, take another five to ten minutes to write down your thoughts. Maybe note the changes you would make to that room, the weather outside, the people or pictures that you saw in your environment. Write down any ideas or thoughts you had, no matter how trivial they may seem to you.

Market Research

Now, you have at least three ideas for an invention, whether it be a product or service. It is easy to fall in love with one of your ideas because it's something that you personally care about and would benefit from as the ideal consumer. However, the only way to know whether your idea is solid and has the potential to generate income is to do thorough market research.

If you are like me and have absolutely zero experience in conducting market research and knowing the right questions to ask, then this part can seem overwhelming and the next roadblock in your path to entrepreneurship. Market research is a mentally taxing and dense challenge. It will require you to identify your target audience, comprehensively investigate those ideal customers, and adjust your idea invention to better fit their needs. Moreover, market research is a task that you will have to revisit time and time again to ensure that you are meeting the market's needs and can still sell your product over time.

Before you begin the labor of inventing a product, take the time to practice reasonable diligence with research. This is especially important if you want to pursue patent protection for your idea. Your research should extend further than whether your friends and family members would purchase your product. You need to ask yourself thoughtful and difficult questions. Such as: Does your design impose on someone else's intellectual property or copyright? What are the differences between a patent, copyright, and trademark?

Many inventors begin their research process with some idea of what defines their target audience. For example, if you have invented a video game, you know that your market is broadly defined by teenagers and adolescents. Or, if you have an idea for new plastic food storage, your market is probably an adult female majority. Yet, you may be surprised by the valuable nuances market research can uncover. You may realize that twenty and thirty-somethings offer greater sales potential for that video game -or that single adult males have a higher need for food storage containers.

Just as important as understanding who your target audience is, is knowing "why" and "what." Customers are getting along just fine without your product. What are they using right now to solve the problem that you have identified? Why would they use your product instead? How much would they have to pay for your product? These questions are the reason why market research is so important. You will always begin with an idea or hypothesis about your target markets, but your research will refine the information and supply feedback on how to potentially improve your invention.

Exercise 4: Write down and identify your target customer, being as specific as possible. Describe their age, gender, family life, priorities, income, etc. In addition, write down what you think is most important to them when it comes to making everyday life easier or less stressful. Finally, describe how your invention would benefit this person.

Creating Your First Product to Test

Now it's time to create the first physical manifestation of your invention. This can be done by either creating a prototype or brochure of your invention or service so potential consumers have something they can objectively judge. You want to give your potential audience an idea of what your product will look like and feel like, as well as its functions and capabilities.

If you create a brochure, you may want to invest in a graphic designer or someone who is skilled with technical drawings. The brochure should be attractive, as it is the initial introduction to your invention. Even with only a brochure, people will use whatever you give them to judge the merits of your product, so the quality of your brochure and the effort you put in to create it will reflect on your overall product. It will be a direct reflection on your invention.

You also have the option of building a prototype of your invention. Throughout the creative process, you should go through several prototypes as you evolve and develop your idea until it is in its final state. However, once again, if your prototype reflects poor effort (made with plywood and duct tape, for example), then people will not respond positively to your idea even if it is a good one.

If you are not someone who is technologically efficient or doesn't know their way around a workshop, you always have the option of hiring a prototype designer who can make an attractive enough example of your invention.

At this point, it is finally time to start thinking about your first prototype in terms of your idea's relation to the marketplace. Even though I had a clear understanding of who my target customer was, I needed to ensure that my first draft fit the market's needs and also had a place within the market.

It was tempting to immediately begin creating my prototype, but considering the limited resources I had and wanting to do my very best, I knew that product creation needed to take a backseat to research. For the first time, I needed to delve deeply into researching everything I could about my customers, competition, and how to use the information I gathered to make my product even better.

However, in order to get the most out of the many hours it takes to get this information, I needed to learn how to efficiently collect data and ask the right questions. This step of the process is often skipped and overlooked, even by the most ambitious and business-savvy creators. We get so caught up in the excitement of inventing that we end up wasting time, money, and resources because the first product doesn't do well when introduced to the market. I know that you're probably itching to get started, so I'll make this part as painless and simple as possible.

Defining Data Types

I'm going to begin by defining the two different types of market research: primary and secondary. Secondary data is the easiest to get because this is the date that already exists on the internet and in books. It is "big-picture" research that will paint a picture of your market potential, population numbers, demographic information, age groups, gender, etc. You can find this information online, in books and magazines, and especially through the government's census data (which is available online).

On the other hand, primary research helps you to fill in the blanks that are left open by secondary research. It typically applies directly to your invention. You can use focus groups, interviews, polling, and other methods to gather primary data in order to determine your market's habits and behaviors as they relate to your invention.

Think of the surveys companies offer to pay you for online, or if you have ever participated in a focus group for a product. You may be shown a commercial or given a sample of the product and then are asked questions to better understand your feelings towards it.

For example, how much you would pay to see a movie you just watched a trailer for, whether you would go to the store for a video game or purchase it online.

When to Revise Your Product

The data that is collected during the primary research phase can direct your invention's evolution and your distribution and marketing strategies. I've met a few creators who completely designed, developed, and manufactured their products only to find that no one is buying their invention after spending a fortune to develop it.

To help you during this crucial point, I have included a few tell-tale signs that show you need to revisit the function of your product and conduct more research.

Disparity

There is a separation between the service or product and the customer.

Many creators go off of the feedback from their family members and friends and believe that their invention simply can't fail. However, data derived only from your social network is lacking and cannot be critically analyzed. Remember Crystal Pepsi, New Coke, or the Amazon Fire Phone?

How to avoid this mistake:

Before mass producing your invention, conduct several focus group tests to ensure that people like and would use your product. The key to hosting a successful focus group is ensuring that your participants are completely candid. You want their honest feedback, including any issues using the product, or if they would make any changes to improve functionality.

Pricing

There is an issue with the price tag.

If the price tag is too high for the problem that your invention aims to solve, then consumers simply won't buy it. This point is especially important to consider because manufacturing costs are often included in price negotiations because they usually directly impact the pricing of the product. If you find that your invention simply costs too much to make and can't sell at a price point that generates profit, then it's time to think of a new idea.

Finding a comfortable price:

No one likes overpaying. Most customers will search for the cheapest option available, looking for the biggest bang for their buck. Customers will look for your product to solve their problem, but won't pay the price if they think it costs too much. After all, they've gone this long without your invention, why pay to solve their issue now? Investigate your competition's products, ask for suggested price points from your focus groups, and consider the costs of mass-producing before putting a price tag on your invention.

Poor Packaging

The packaging doesn't hit the mark.

The packaging on your product should clarify exactly what your product does. It also needs to be engaging and bright so that it doesn't get lost on store shelves. Most customers don't spend the five minutes it takes to read a paragraph of explanation on the back of a product, so you need to make that first impression count.

Fool-proof packaging:

Your packaging should be both eye-catching and representative of your brand. However, it should also effortlessly and effectively communicate your invention's purpose. If your product is completely new and different from anything else on the market, your potential customers won't know what they are looking at. Your product's features, functions, and benefits should be clearly outlined on your packaging. Your packaging should answer these three questions:

1. What features make this product unique?

2. What problems does the product solve for your target customer?

3. How will it improve or benefit my customer's life?

Similarities

There is a product on the market that is already doing well and filling the customer's needs.

It doesn't matter whether your invention is original or patented; if it is too similar to a product consumers are already using, they won't see the value in buying your product too.

Know your competition:

Your test groups and market should be able to tell you if there is another product out there that they believe solves the same problem your invention does. You should need to know whether your target customers are already using your competitor's alternative. Once you have identified your competition's product, find out what its strengths and weaknesses are and how your solution is different.

A perfect example is the invention of the small spiked balls you put into the clothes dryer in place of dryer sheet fabric softeners. Both the spiked balls and dryer sheets solve the problems of combating static electricity and making ironing easier. But the spiked balls are friendlier to the environment because they are reusable, they decrease drying time, and save customers more money in the long run. This is the type of information you can uncover through market research.

Tips for Bringing Your Idea to Life: Creating the Prototype

Coherency and Minimalism

This is not the time to overcomplicate your invention and its purpose. Having a cohesive and rational idea with minimum components will help you develop your prototype quickly. Your invention can be as creative as you would like, but your pre-prototype ideas and drawings should be clean and simple to help quicken the creative process.

It is tempting to bring your idea to life as fast as possible, especially when making a profit is one of your most urgent goals. But ultimately, you want your idea to be sound and successful. Keeping the prototype process as minimal and to the point as you can will help clarify the vision of your business and your product's functions.

Restricting Your Creativity to Spark Better Ideas

Start by writing down a list of just twenty features and functions you have in mind for your invention. Next, choose the top five from the list and make those the priority, completely avoiding the other fifteen features on your list. You want to limit yourself so that you are forced to focus on the greater benefits and functionality of your product, without getting sidetracked by all the other ideas and possibilities that you can come up with. You don't want to waste additional time and resources by focusing on a less important aspect of your invention.

It Doesn't Have to be Perfect

The founder of LinkedIn, Reid Hoffman, once said, "if you are not embarrassed by the first version of your product, you've launched too late." Your first prototype doesn't have to be perfect. Spending all of your time and money trying to get it right the first time is going to stunt your progress and keep you in the prototype phase longer than necessary. Just make the first version of your invention and roll with it.

There is never going to be a 'right time' to pursue your idea, you will never feel one hundred percent ready or confident. As some of the greatest entrepreneurs have said, "fail fast and fail often." Failing faster means that you are able to get back to development and testing, helping you reach your final product faster than you would have by spending more time in the prototype phase.

Learn and Practice the 4 P's of Marketing

The marketing mix and the four P's of marketing are typically used as synonyms for each other. However, they are not always the same thing. Yet, if you understand the four P's of marketing, then you can make your product better and get it on store shelves sooner. The term "marketing mix" is generally used to describe the different kinds of decisions companies have to make throughout the process of introducing a product or service to the market. The four P's is considered the best-known way of defining the market mix and is the most widely practiced method of product development.

The four P's are as follows:

1. Product/Service

2. Place

3. Price

4. Promotion

I've created a series of questions to help you identify your product's four P's to better define your marketing mix. And yes, once again, you should definitely be writing down these questions and your answers so you can apply them to your product's development.

Product/Service

- What does your target consumer want from your invention? What specific needs or wants does it fulfill?

- What features does your invention have to meet the needs you just defined?

- Are there features you can add to better meet your consumer's needs?

- Does your invention have features that your consumer won't actually use?

- How and where will your consumer use your invention?

- What will your invention look like? Think of this question in terms of design, color, shape, size, etc. How does its appearance contribute to the function of the product?

- What is the name of your product, and how will it be branded?

- How is your invention different from your competitor's, and where does it fit in the marketplace?

- What will it cost for you to produce this product while still generating a profit?

Place

- Where would customers look for your invention in order to buy it?

- If you are selling your product in a store, in what kind of store would you sell it? (Online, grocery stores, convenience stores, boutiques?)

- How can you access the right distribution channels? (Do you want your customers to speak with a salesperson, order online, or have a customer service line they can call?)

- What are your competitors doing in terms of product placement? How can you learn from your competition or differentiate from them?

Price

- What is the true value of your product to the customer?

- Are there price points already established for this type of product or service within the market?

- Is your target customer price sensitive? Will a small increase or decrease in price help you gain extra market share?

- What discounts can be offered to trade customers?

- How does your price tag compare with that of your competition?

Promotion

- Where and when can you amplify your marketing messages to reach your target customers?

- How will you advertise your product or service to your audience? (Online, on television, using billboards, direct marketing mail?)

- When is the best time for you to promote your invention? Is it a seasonal product that should only be offered for a limited time?

- How is your competition promoting similar products? How do their promotions affect your choice of promotional effort?

Chapter 2: Prototypes and Product Testing

A great idea is only as good as the execution behind it. You now have at least one idea for a product or service, but now it's time to manifest it into something that you can see and touch. Unfortunately, this is one of those turning points in the process when only the strongest are able to surpass the challenges that are at the forefront of prototype development.

One of the most essential early steps in the creation process is inventing a prototype. Defined accurately, a prototype is a three-dimensional adaption of your concept. Creating a prototype can be one of the most enjoyable and rewarding parts of the invention journey.

This is because developing a prototype allows you the opportunity to dive deep into your creativity and use the skills that inspired you to invent an idea in the first place. Whether you are sitting at a kitchen table drawing sketches or in a workshop with all the materials you need, whether you are a stay-at-home parent or a full-time engineer, the most exciting part of the process is watching your idea transform into something real and tangible.

If you're someone who has never created a physical product before, you may be wondering what a prototype of your idea should look like. Of course, the answer is that it depends on what your idea is. Secondly, it depends on what your budget and goals are. The first step that I like to take, because it is the simplest and easiest, is to use household items to create something handmade.

It doesn't matter how rudimentary the first prototype looks, if it works for your initial demonstration, then everyday items like socks, glue, and empty egg cartons are as good as the most expensive craft materials money can buy. If you make the decision to move forward with your invention, this first prototype will eventually become known as a "pre-production" prototype. Regardless, a homemade model and basic presentation can give you a great running start.

Why Prototype?

You may be asking yourself, "why is making a prototype so important if I know exactly what I want?" While prototyping may seem like a waste of time, especially if you have built inventions, models, and larger projects, there are several important reasons why it is a necessary step.

To Test and Refine

It gives you the opportunity to test and refine the functionality of your invention.

Your idea and design might work in theory, but you won't notice the flaws in your product until you start physically creating it. Having a prototype also allows you to test the functionality of your invention. Sometimes you don't realize how many issues your design has until you are confronted with those challenges. For the product I created, I genuinely believed that I had struck gold with the resources I used for my first prototype. It turned out that the product didn't work as well as other options and went through several formulas and prototypes to finally get the result I needed. Which brings me to my next point.

Test Materials

Building a prototype lets you test the performance of different materials.

There are dozens of resources out there, metals, plastic, rubber, etc. I know that it can be a challenge to let go of your original plan because you invested a lot of time and energy into your invention. However, testing various materials will help you find the best method for constructing your product. This also goes for ideas that provide services rather than products. With the advanced technology we have available to us, testing several methods of customer service, delivery, payments, etc. will help you find the most efficient method of creating your business.

Literal Description

This will allow you to describe your invention more adequately to get the desired end result.

Passion can only take you so far in the business world. You need to be able to describe the specific functions and design of your prototype to help sell your idea to your team. This includes your attorney, potential investors, business partners, marketers, manufacturers, and engineers.

Shows Earnestness

Having a prototype strengthens your rapport and forces others to take your invention seriously.

Trust me, with many people on your social media profile advertising their own side hustles to get business, your invention will seem like another network marketing money grab. This is something that you are serious and passionate about. A prototype will help others see that you have thought this venture through and are making it a reality. Arriving at meetings with a prototype in hand will separate you from the dozens of other entrepreneurs who can only offer vague ideas. You need to stand out from everyone else to give your invention a leg to stand on.

Planning a Prototype

In 2015, the United States Patent and Trademark Office processed over six hundred thousand patent applications. However, only fifty-five percent of those applicants received patents. While pursuing creative ownership and licensing may seem like a far-off goal, one of the best ways to improve your odds of getting a patent grant is to develop your first prototype. Submitting a prototype is not required by the U. S. Patent Office upon sending in your application, it does serve the purpose of demonstrating that you have put a lot of thought and effort into your idea, which will merit greater consideration.

Concept Sketch

Always start with a concept sketch.

Before you can turn your idea into a reality, you have to get it down on paper first. Drawing your idea will help you visualize your end product in greater detail, especially when you have dozens of ideas and concepts running through your head. I always keep a sketch notebook, because it provides additional documentation of my creative process for when I submit my patent applications.

Having a sketch notebook will also come in handy later on if you ever need to defend your rightful ownership over your intellectual property. But more on that later. I know that there are a ton of digital drawing computer programs out there that you can use to start the drafting process. However, hand-drawn sketches have been shown to carry more weight in court than electronically produced sketches.

Digital Sketch

After you have developed a prototype sketch, you need to create a digital sketch of your invention.

You can use a standard digital design program that allows you to make 2-D and 3-D depictions. Having a 3-D image of your product lets you rotate and animate your virtual drawing, so you can see your invention from every angle. If you're not tech-savvy, then you can hire a professional graphic designer or prototype designer to help make your sketch into a digitized rendering.

Building a Prototype

Now it's time to create a physical prototype. There are two routes you can take: building one yourself or hiring a professional prototype designer or engineer. From my own experience, I believe that when you have finally developed your prototype as far as you reasonably can, it is time to consult with a professional.

As an inventor who started with a small budget and limited resources, I know firsthand how invaluable an expert's opinion is. The complexity and materials of your design will drive the decision to hire the right person to partner with -a machinist, industrial design student, carpenter, handyman, or engineer.

There are several other resources you can use to your advantage to get the most out of this part of the process. If you are strapped for cash, you can post on websites like Facebook Marketplace, Craigslist, Yellow Pages, and similar forums to enlist the help of handymen and designers.

Keep in mind that the first few prototypes serve the purpose of helping you to identify the flaws and kinks in your invention. The prototyping stage is an opportunity to tap into your creative ability and challenge the other consumer options that are on the market. You should consider researching new and emerging technologies in designing the final product.

Using a 3-D Printer

One uncommon method of building a prototype is investing in a 3-D printer. This is because this technology is not just new, but also expensive. The cheapest models you can find are priced around $200.00, while higher quality models can range between $700.00 to $2,000.

However, one of the greatest benefits of using a 3-D printer is being able to rapidly turn your idea into a product in just a day. You are also able to efficiently customize your designs and have an immediate prototype to test and develop, which speeds up the prototyping process by a considerable amount.

If you can't fit a 3-D printer into your budget, you also have the option of hiring a third party to print your invention for you. Websites like www.cubify.com allow you to upload a CAD (computer-aided design) file to the site, where it will allow you to choose what material you would like your prototype to be built from (like ceramic or metal for example), and then you will receive your product in the mail.

Deconstruct the Competition

Unless you have come up with a completely original idea, your invention is going to have competitors in the market.

However, this could be the stage when the competition could actually benefit you. If you are struggling with the logistics of your product's design, then you can buy your competition's products and disassemble them to understand how they work.

If you're building a children's toy, find a similar toy and take it apart to look at the materials that make it work. Of course, you should never copy someone else's design, that's just asking to get sued. But, you can teach yourself how to make electronics work, computer coding, app building, and many other skills that can help you create your product.

Don't Aim for Perfection

As much as you may wish, there is absolutely no way that your first prototype will be perfect. For me, this was the most difficult mental challenge for me to overcome. When you have put in so much work and effort just to make your prototype function, the last thing you want to do is begin the process all over again and pick apart your product's flaws. It's okay for your prototype to have issues or not look the way you originally planned.

The purpose of the prototype is:

- to evaluate your idea
- validate your design's functionality
- improve your invention until it is perfect

Exercise 1: List three materials that you can use to build your product. Additionally, write out the core functions of your product and the solution that it provides users.

Testing Your Prototype: Taking the Next Step

Once you have built the prototype, it's time to show it off. Direct customer feedback is the best way that you can test your product because these are the people that will eventually invest their money into your invention. The first few rounds of testing are going to give you the most feedback, including criticism. Therefore, learning from your prototypes and test subjects is essential in saving you time and resources during the development phase.

You want to move quickly and efficiently while testing your product, gathering feedback, and immediately working to create solutions to any problems and improving on your idea to get the desired end result. In order to help you maximize learning from your tests, I've gathered the best practice tips on gathering and organizing your feedback.

Soliciting Feedback

How you solicit feedback from your product testers is mostly dependent on the type of invention you have created. For example, if the prototype requires the user to role-play a scenario in order to achieve the desired result, other variables will come into play. For instance, if you have produced an alternative to sponges for scrubbing dishes, the user would have to test your product on several types of dishware, use different dish soaps, etc. Keep in mind that you will need several people to test your product.

As you are going through the testing process, you want to get the best feedback possible. This means generalized, simple statements won't do. Most people tend to hold back their negative comments because they don't want to hurt your feelings. However, this part of the process can either expedite prototyping or derail your progress. You want to get solid, detailed, critical feedback -even from your family and friends.

Another general rule of thumb to follow to gain useful feedback is to bring several prototypes to compare. Whether they differ in color or function, offering more than one option will give you critical feedback on specific likes and dislikes for each version, and will give your test subjects the push to be more honest.

Lastly, in collecting valuable feedback, you may want to use the "I Like, I Wish, What If" method. This strategy encourages your feedback group to follow a more structured approach when providing commentary, taking on a critical yet positive manner as they evaluate your invention. The method requires the user to use three different statements to communicate their feelings.

"I like..." The first statement encourages the user to say something positive about your product.

"**I wish...**" This second statement prompts the tester to share their ideas of how the prototype can be improved so that it addresses a personal concern for the customer. The "I wish" assertion allows the tester to provide direct, constructive, negative feedback.

"**What if...**" The last statement inspires new suggestions from the tester that may not have a direct link to your invention. While this may seem like the least helpful part of the process, it actually allows you to think of new ideas for future iterations for your invention.

Exercise 2: Write five questions that you can ask future test groups, including one question about their personal use of the product and one question about additional functions the product could have in solving their problem.

Testing Your Invention with the Right People

Whom you test your invention on will directly correlate with the usefulness and relevance of their feedback. When you are in the early stages of design and development, rough and simple criticism will be good enough to keep your creative gears turning to continuously build better versions of your invention. However, as your project comes to an end and your prototypes become more detailed, and near the final product, you will want to increase the range of users to get the most relevant and insightful feedback.

One way that you can optimize your testing is by putting extreme users to the test, on top of typical customers. Think of your customer base in terms of a spectrum, I'll use grocery store shoppers as an example. On one end of the spectrum, you have extreme users who shop at the grocery store every day.

On the other end of the spectrum are the people who never shop at grocery stores. Testing your prototypes on extreme consumers will help you discover relevant problems that will ultimately affect regular customers. Working with more passionate buyers will also lead to a more candid response, as extreme users tend to be more vocal when they care about the product they are testing.

If you are debuting a product or service that is international or crosses regional lines, then you need to consider testing your prototypes in several regions and countries. Keep in mind that cultural differences and customs could affect how people around the world use your invention.

Upon the final stages of your project, you should ask for feedback from stakeholders in your invention. Internal stakeholders within your creative team, distributors, and manufacturers will have their own opinions and standards for building, packaging, and shipping a product. Their input can add to the level of success you achieve with your idea. Collecting feedback from your stakeholders in the final stages of prototyping will also prevent any monetary, mechanical, production, and distribution issues with your final prototype.

Be an Unbiased Party and Adapt Willingly

It's easy to get caught up in the emotional ties to your prototype, but adhering to an unbiased presentation of your invention will ultimately benefit your progress. Remember that prototyping and testing are about uncovering new ways to improve your invention.

Attempting to oversell your product can prove to be detrimental to this goal. When hearing others voice negative comments, remain level-headed, and refrain from acting defensive. Your course of action should be probing them further to find out what they would specifically improve on and propose solutions to problems they find.

Avoid becoming too attached to the product and always be willing to change, deconstruct, and even forget about the idea if and when the time comes.

Prototyping is like a rehearsal for your prototype, cutting out the parts that don't contribute to the overall purpose so that you don't get destroyed in the actual marketplace. You may come to a point where certain components start distracting from the core functions of your product.

You need to be able to adapt quickly and efficiently to consumer demands and take their feedback to heart. During your testing sessions, you should allow and encourage your test subjects to contribute to the conversation.

As the future buyers of your invention, they know exactly what problems your product will solve and suggest solutions that you may have never thought of. This will contribute to greater success later on when you finally enter the market.

Exercise 3: List four ways that you can improve your product, including the design, sub-functions, core functions, and overall effectiveness.

Gather Feedback and Keep Trying

Gathering feedback from users during the prototype phase is absolutely useless if you don't use the information to create the next iteration of your idea.

You need to continuously integrate what you learn from the users into your newer designs as you move forward. As you build new renditions of your product, you can conduct post-feedback discussions with your development team -

using the same methods of questioning that you utilized with test subjects.

The people that you partner with to bring this idea to life should be your soundboard throughout the development process. They should be helping you brainstorm new designs and functions, and supporting you as you aggressively take action to make your idea a reality.

Keep developing your prototypes, and constantly test them until you eventually arrive at an optimal solution.

What Comes Next?

In the next chapter, we're going to explore the stage of bringing your invention from an idea to a real-life product: patenting. Perhaps the most important step in this entire process is protecting your rightful property, in all its forms. You will learn the difference between copyrights, trademarks, and patents, as well as legal tips and finding a factory to produce your invention.

Chapter 3: Patents and Manufacturing

Congratulations! You have successfully invented a product and brought it to life! This next chapter will explain the importance of protecting your invention, as well as how to find a factory that will mass produce your product. There is a general lack of understanding when it comes to protecting ideas and inventions, even in the business world. However, as an innovator, you do have basic legal protections.

Here's an example of how legal protection can save you later on. A small company in the state of Ohio made almost $300,000 by selling its patented speed control device to a few Fortune 500 companies. However, almost immediately, another business copied the idea and started selling their copycat in the same market. The original company in Ohio filed a lawsuit claiming patent infringement.

Unfortunately, the original company made one of the greatest mistakes that can be made by any new business or entrepreneur. They neglected to file a patent application until thirteen months after shipping out its first order of over one thousand units. The one year delay violated a law that requires patents to be filed within twelve months after the first sale of a product. The end result? The court invalidated the patent and ordered the original company to pay its rival's attorney's fees.

Another valuable example of a young company's costly negligence is when a Minnesota food company was the first to adopt the phrase "Old Dutch" as a trademark, based on a saying that is common in the upper Midwest. While immediately acquiring a federal trademark registration would have protected the company's exclusive rights to use the "Old Dutch" trademark, the filing was delayed, and an East Coast food company copied the name. The unfortunate result was the East Coast Company establishing exclusive rights to the trademark in six eastern states.

Just these two examples serve to show how valuable ideas from small businesses are frequently taken away by the competition -without any consequence to the copycat. But if you take the right and necessary legal actions to protect your ideas, then you can continue taking creative leadership in the market. But, unless you are a lawyer or practiced businessman, then you probably aren't familiar with the ins and outs of patenting and copyright. There are five fundamental and vital legal tools for safeguarding inventions: patents, copyrights, trademarks, trade secrets, and trade dress unfair competition laws.

Patents

By definition, a patent is a form of intellectual property that grants the owner legal ownership to prevent outside parties from creating, selling, using, and importing an invention for a limited number of years. Inventions that meet the standards for patenting include a product, man-made microorganisms, a method, a computer program, and an apparatus. In order to qualify for the right to a patent, the owner has to file an application describing the invention or product in the United States Patent and Trademark Office.

After the office establishes that the invention is indeed new, it will release the patent. This process can take up to two years, another reason why you should file for a patent as soon as possible. The patent establishes exclusive rights, for example, the right to sue to stop other parties from utilizing your invention and collecting damages for an unapproved use. However, these rights do not begin until after the patent is issued.

Patents don't just cover major advances, but also less obvious future improvements. It may be in your favor to apply for a patent on such improvements, simply to put in the phrase "patent" or "patent pending" on your invention, its packaging, and marketing. Putting "patent" or "patent pending" on advertisements and packaging lets the public know that your product is exclusive and original.

The next time you watch television, keep an eye out for product commercials, like a Mr. Coffee electric coffee maker, you'll see that the company highlights the uniqueness of their product in advertisements by stating that the design is patented. By applying for a patent, you are securing a greater level of professionalism as an inventor and adding another benefit to display in your product's marketing.

There are a few basic requirements to fulfill to ensure your patent rights. You should always consult with a patent attorney. Before seeking legal advice, you need to be careful not to release any details about your invention, especially on a public level. Public disclosure of any information triggers several laws by which your rights as an inventor can be permanently lost. In addition, you should also obtain written documentation of every step that went into creating your invention, signed by a witness, to show as evidence that you are the true inventor.

While it's a difficult thing to think about, you should always be watchful of your employees or any partners you are working with. If any of your staff members are inventors as well, you need to have them sign agreements before working for you, stating that any inventions that are developed during their time working with you belong to you. This adds another level of protection. You have spent a lot of time and money to get to this point, and there is no such thing as being too careful when it comes to ensuring your ideas are completely protected. There is no such thing as automatic or assumed patents.

Be aware that it may take several years before your patent is granted. However, until that decision is made of whether you are granted a patent, your idea will be protected. A patent can protect your invention for up to twenty years, giving you the exclusive rights to your idea for creating, using, and selling the design and product, as well as the importing rights.

Provisional Patent Applications

A provisional patent is another tool that you can use to your advantage. A provisional patent application can be used to secure a patent filing date while sidestepping the costs that are associated with the filing and prosecution process of a traditional patent application. If a non-provisional application is submitted within twelve months from the filing date of a provisional patent application, the submission date of the nonprovisional application will take on the filing date of the provisional application.

There are several differences between a provisional patent application and a regular or non-provisional patent. One of the biggest differences is that a provisional patent application is not reviewed. The provisional patent application is used to avoid paying the costs that are associated with a typical patent application (like the application and attorney's fees) for one year while taking the time to determine whether your invention is commercially feasible. The provisional patent application is not made public unless the application number is later noted in the true patent or a future published application.

The United States is a first to file nation. This means that inventors need to file the patent first before disclosing any details regarding their invention, offering to sell their invention, or using their invention in a public setting. A provisional patent application costs around $140.00, while a non-provisional patent application costs about $730.00. Remember that if you choose to pursue the route of a provisional patent application, you only have twelve months before you absolutely must file a non-provisional application to complete the patent filing process. There are no extensions or exceptions.

Trade Secrets Law

If your invention does not qualify for a patent, there is no need to panic or get discouraged. You can still seek protection for your idea under the trade secrets law, as long as it falls within the qualifications. Trade secrets are pieces of information, which can include: a formula, program, process, pattern, technique, compilation, method, or device. In order to meet the basic definition of a trade secret, your invention has to be used in business, and have the capability of obtaining an economic advantage over the other competitors within the market who don't know this secret exists.

Think of it in terms of Coca-Cola's soda recipe -it is still a valuable and heavily guarded secret. Trade secrets are defined as all the documents and bits of information within a business that the company takes extra precautions to conceal from outside entities, which are not up for sale nor disclosed upon the sale of the company's products. Some examples include client lists, recipes, blueprints, etc. The business's ownership in these confidential pieces of information exists upon their invention.

While there isn't an application that needs to be filed, maintaining secrecy is vital. A business cannot prevent an outside source from using the secret if the owner or anyone else representing the business is voluntarily or negligently revealing it without having the outsider sign a non-disclosure agreement first. You also cannot keep an outsider from taking advantage of any trade secrets if the outsider figures it out for themselves, without any prior knowledge of it.

Trade secrets are typically for protecting internal matters and are often used in the advertising of a product to flash its exclusivity in a product or invention. Think of commercials for beauty products. They often boast about secret formulas or ingredients that guarantee an otherwise unachievable result.

If the fundamental requirements to maintain trade secret rights are preserved, then your invention's information can be protected indefinitely. Once again, using Coca-Cola as the prime example, its soda formula has been protected and hidden for almost a hundred years.

One of the criteria for meeting trade secret standards is having a person sign an agreement promising they will keep the secret before giving them access to the said trade secret. For example, staff and hired independent consultants hold a responsibility to not reveal trade secrets. Federal laws that govern such responsibilities are not necessarily clear, especially when it comes to staff members when they no longer work for the company.

This means that all employees should be required to sign a secrecy agreement upon beginning their employment with you. Secrecy agreements will also prove valuable should another company come into possession of your secret without authorization. In order for your invention to fall under the protection of trade secret law, you must also have a sensible and reliable in-house control process that secures any secret documents from outsiders. If another company or outside party misappropriates your company's secret, a court can order that competitor to pay you royalties, damages, court costs, and attorney's fees.

Trademarks

A trademark is defined as a type of intellectual property that makes up a recognizable design, word, symbol, sign, phrase or expression which identifies products or services of a specific company that sets them apart from others. The owner of a trademark can be a person, legal entity, organization, or business. Just like patents, trademarks can be used to your advantage in your advertising and marketing strategy.

Identifying characteristics that can qualify for trademark protection include:

Shape

The shape of a product, like a Coca-Cola bottle, Toblerone's triangular chocolate, Hershey Kisses, and Pringle's Potato Chips.

Building Design

The design of a company's building, like McDonald's golden arches, Apple's technology stores, New York City's Empire State Building, and India's Taj Mahal Palace.

Ornamental Color or Design

The decoration of a product, like the black and gold design of a Duracell battery, the red soles of Christian Louboutin shoes, or Nike sneakers. This protection also extends to specific colors, such as Tiffany Blue, Barbie Pink, Target Red, UPS Brown, and Cadbury Purple.

Phrases

You can probably think of a dozen of these catchy phrases off the top of your head, but here are a few examples to give you a better idea. McDonald's "I'm lovin' it," boxing announcer Michael Buffer's "Let's get ready to rumble!" Taylor Swift's "This sick beat," and even Donald Trump's famous line from his television show The Apprentice, "You're fired."

Symbols

This is the big one, a company's marketing department has done an excellent job branding their product or business if consumers can recognize their company just by their symbol or logo. Examples of logos and symbols include the Starbucks Mermaid, Batman's Bat-Signal, Pepsi's blue, red, and white circle, and television network NBC's Rainbow Peacock.

In order to establish sole ownership over a trademark, you first have to use it in a commercial sale of your product or service. Immediately afterward, you need to file an application for registration of the mark through the United States Patent and Trademark Office https://www.uspto.gov/.

The Patent and Trademark Office will then determine whether the mark is not easily confused with or similar to any other previously registered mark. Then, they will issue the official registration to you. Just as you may have assumed, a trademark notice establishes your rights to legally prevent anyone else from using the mark anywhere in the country, even if they didn't know that you own the trademark.

Fundamental requirements to claim trademark rights include investigating to see if the mark is available, getting legal advice to verify that the design or mark can be registered, and learning how to use a mark correctly to solidify your ownership of it. If you consult with a trademark attorney, they can check the Patent and Trademark Office or private computer search company that can search federal and state registrations.

If you have designed a mark that is identifiable to your product or service, you are not required to register the trademark for protection. Simply using your trademark grants you the rights to it. Although, from past experience, I can guarantee that you want the benefits of having legal ownership.

With trademark registration, the public is notified that you are the owner of the trademark. The law assumes that the mark is yours and grants you exclusive rights to use the mark on any goods or services that are detailed in the application. Once you have the trademark, you have ownership over it for up to ten years at a time.

Copyrights

A copyright is the absolute legal right given to a creator to print, perform, record, film, or publish artistic, literary, or musical material, as well as give permission to other people to do the same. A copyright prohibits the copying of any work of art, computer program, or writing. Ownership over a printed work automatically exists the moment the creation is made into a tangible form. A tangible form can take any shape, like that of a video or voice recording, music notes, or lyrics on a piece of paper, really anything physical that allows you to claim original ownership.

It should be clarified that any ownership of overwriting or art can be forfeited if the work is shown publicly without legitimate notice. Proper notice can include the © symbol, the year the work was first made public, and the name of the owner included with the displayed work. A copyright can be legally registered before or after production, with the filing of an application through the Copyright Office of the United States Library of Congress https://www.copyright.gov/.

Copyrights cover many written texts, like pamphlets, journals, and books. However, the laws will also protect practically all written and artwork material that is utilized in advertising and marketing campaigns. This means that your package design, printed and published advertisements, sales scripts, operation manuals, and instruction manuals. The copyright laws also extend to materials and products, such as clothing designs, belt buckles, furniture designs, and the like.

Unlike trademarks, copyrights are immediately and automatically existent upon the creation of the invention. However, if this is the route you choose as the inventor, then you still need to ensure those rights are protected and preserved. This means giving proper notice (as described above) whenever that work is shown in a public space. You should seek federal registration on any important piece you create in case you need to prove your ownership in an infringement suit. Businesses that are mass producing copyrighted works (like greeting cards or app designers) can save money by omitting federal restrictions on copyrights until it becomes apparent that their creation will become important.

If you seek to hire freelancers for product development, before they begin working on the project, you must have them agree that the product is not their property, but yours. Otherwise, the author or original artist has total control over the project, including the disposal of the said project.

In seeking registration for material produced, you should always send a copy of your work along with the processing fee. The duration period for a copyrighted work will vary depending on the date the work was created and registered. However, the typical copyright laws cover the extent of an author's life, plus seventy years.

Trade Dress Unfair Competition Laws

In addition to seeking protection under federal law with patents, trademarks, and copyrights, you can also use state common law protections, such as trade dress unfair competition laws. The phrase "trade dress" alludes to the distinctive way the product is designed and packaged. This includes the labels, color scheme, and advertisements on the product.

Trade dress unfair competition laws protect you from unauthorized copying of ornamental and unique package and product designs, anything decorative that does not contribute to the functional features of the product. Similar to some trademark examples I gave previously in this chapter, the ornamental features that protect your product should serve the purpose of being recognized by the public as a design exclusive to your product. And just like the copyright laws, the right granted through the trade dress unfair competition laws automatically exists without needing to file an application, just as soon as your product or service receives public recognition.

Unlike trademarks, although similarities do overlap between the two, unfair competition includes a broader scope of design possibilities. There are designs that are protected by the courts but do not qualify for trademark protection. For example, a mattress-cover design, color-coded organizational systems, or distinctive color schemes for cars.

While there isn't an application to file that will preserve trade dress unfair competition rights, there are a few guidelines that will help your invention meet the requirements for protection. The best piece of advice I can offer is to create a distinctive and unique invention and package designs for your product as soon as you can. Then, use marketing strategies to publicize your product so that you can publicly claim rightful ownership.

Depending on what your invention is, some ideas may need protection from more than one type of legal coverage. If you register your invention in the United States, then you have the privilege of protection from treaties and agreements that will make international selling and distribution much easier.

If any type of violation with your copyright, trademark, or patent occurs overseas, then the respective government agencies will refrain from getting involved. It will be up to the individuals or companies to reach an agreement. Regardless of which route of protection you choose to take, you should save early drafts of your work, as well as detailed records of product development and who you've shared your ideas with.

Guidelines for Additional Protection

It's natural to be afraid that your ideas or inventions might be stolen. When I first started developing my product, I made sure that I only told my significant other about the idea. I didn't want to risk my idea getting out there and possibly being stolen, even though I was sure I could trust all of my friends and family. Truth be told, good ideas don't come by the dozens. It took me a year to think of my product, develop it, and start thinking about packaging.

I didn't want my hard work compromised because someone I trust has loose lips. Instead, I kept my head down and waited until my invention was legally protected until I finally told anyone else about it. There are too many cases out there of ideas being stolen from good people, like the Candy Crush Saga, Facebook, and Snapchat. It's best to protect your ideas and keep your inner circle small until you are certain you have legal coverage.

During the development process, you are going to want to ask for help from an industry expert. After all, who would know better than someone with real business experience? You'll also need to work with a manufacturer or distributor as well. Obtaining a patent can cost thousands of dollars and take months, if not years, to be issued. As a small business owner and inventor, I know that you can't afford to wait that long to bring your idea or services to market. That's why I've compiled an additional list of tools and strategies you can use to your advantage, even in your early development phases.

Do your research.

Before you collaborate with anyone new, whether it is an individual or another company, do as much research as you can about them. Do they have a clean track record? Are there any complaints, legitimate or unconfirmed, about their business practices? Try to find out as much as you can about who they are and how they have handled business collaborations in the past.

Someone I consider a really good friend knows a business leader in our community who generally has a decent reputation with his cohorts. But, I knew that local residents who don't fall within his income bracket have experienced backhanded construction deals, in which he ended up cheating a lot of people out of land and money. Regardless of what my friend said, I conducted my own research on the guy and found out that he was involved in half a dozen lawsuits in several states.

The moral of the story? It doesn't matter what a person's reputation is or what good deeds a business has done in the past. You can't solely trust someone else's judgment when it comes to finding potential partners. If you find someone you trust, but uncover a cause for concern, then consider asking them about it. As we all know by now, not everything you hear or find on the internet is true. But in my opinion, if someone's business practices seem shady before you have even started working with them, then that's a red flag.

Non-Disclosure Agreement (NDA)

An NDA is a mutual agreement between two people to not share specific information with anyone else. An NDA can also go one way if you are sharing information about your invention with someone else. A non-disclosure agreement is a legally binding contract that outlines confidential material, knowledge, and information that at least two parties want to share, but also restrict access to. A few familiar examples of NDA's include doctor-patient confidentiality, priest-penitent privilege, and attorney-client privilege. You can determine the terms and conditions together, as well as the expiration date of the contract.

Non-Compete Agreement

A non-compete agreement, also known as a non-compete clause or covenant not to compete, is an agreement in which one person (typically an employee) agrees not to enter into a similar profession or competing business against their employer (or the other party in the agreement). A non-compete agreement should always be used when hiring a long-term employee and contracted workers.

Work for Hire Agreement

Before taking on a project with an independent contractor or freelancer, you should have a work for hire agreement written and signed so that both parties are protected and agree on all aspects of the development process. A work for hire agreement typically includes a timeline for the project's completion, a comprehensive work schedule, product milestones, and payment negotiations.

This type of contract ensures that the contractor your hire doesn't retain any rights over your invention. Without a legitimized agreement in place, the rights to a project or invention may not be transferred to the client who paid for the work. This type of agreement is often used when hiring artists, graphic designers, and writers for one-off projects. However, even if you have a work for hire agreement, you will still be required to list the contractor or anyone else who contributed any improvements to the invention as co-inventors in the patent application. But, they will still have no rights to your idea or product.

Manufacturing Your Product

You finally have a product, and you've solidified your legal rights and ownership over your invention. Now, it's time to start manufacturing your invention to sell to the public. Unfortunately, this exciting step doesn't come with an exact formula, there is no right answer when it comes to manufacturing in the United States or overseas. Your decision will ultimately come down to your budget, the type of product you're making, personal preference, and patience.

To Outsource or Not to Outsource?

"Outsourcing" has been the golden word for business and emerging entrepreneurs for at least the last decade. Nearly every industry outsources in some way, whether its customer service, manufacturing, labor, or packaging, there doesn't seem to be any problem that outsourcing can't solve, making the process cheaper along the way.

Both the United States and abroad options offer their own challenges. Unfortunately, the globalization effort and a consistently disintegrating American factory base, it isn't always easy or possible to find a factory in the States that can make the product you want.

One of the greatest advantages of making your product in the United States is that it may appeal more to your target audience, many consumers respond better when products are manufactured wholly in the States. Another benefit of using American factories to make your product is that they allow you to order goods in smaller quantities, whereas factories in China require that you place large orders.

It is also worth noting the benefits of having a facility in close proximity to your business. While choosing a cheaper manufacturer has obvious monetary advantages, a well-developed and strong relationship with your factory comes with its own leverage. You can check in on a manufacturing plant that is 50 -200 miles away.

But you can't fly to China, India, or Thailand to make sure that your needs are being met and to resolve any issues that may arise. You will have put in the extra effort to ensure that the logistics of production and distribution are working smoothly, or you'll be risking the quality of your invention.

If you choose to work with a manufacturer outside of the United States, then quality should be your priority. I know of entrepreneurs who worked with manufacturing facilities overseas and were constantly monitoring quality control because it was the biggest issue they had to deal with. While cheap labor and production help with your budget now, you probably don't have the money to spend on flying back and forth to China every other month.

What it comes down to is solid data and real numbers. This means that when you are testing your prototypes with focus groups, you need to ask them whether the location of production is important to them, and if it affects their decision to buy the product. You also need to research the price and quality of the materials and match them with several other factories you're considering before making your decision. In the end, thorough research will decrease the chances of you getting blindsided by a production plant that underdelivers.

Finding a Factory

Finding a factory to produce your invention can seem like an increasingly daunting task. Unless you have experience in product production, then chances are you have very little knowledge of what to look for when choosing which plant to work with. To help you start your search off on the right foot, here are a few online resources you can use towards your advantage.

Maker's Row https://makersrow.com/

Maker's Row is a U. S. -based company that was launched in 2012 by Matthew Burnett, Tanya Menendez, and Scoot Weiner. Menendez realized that they could create a resource that made American factories more accessible. With over 1,400 factories listed on its site, Maker's Row connects you with small, medium-sized, and product-based state-side plants. And if you are still having trouble finding the right match for your needs, you can pay for one-on-one personalized guidance.

Global Sourcing Specialists
http://www.productgss.com/

This company helps match you with a plant that fits your needs and vision from anywhere in the world. Global Sourcing Specialists specifically works with small businesses and startups to locate and manage factories that can produce quality products. You have the benefit of filtering through plants both on U.S. soil and abroad. One of the biggest advantages you have with using Global Sourcing Specialists is that they will negotiate the terms and price for you, to make sure that you get the best deal.

Alibaba https://www.alibaba.com/

If you have your heart set on enlisting the help from an overseas factory, then Alibaba is a great resource to use. With over twenty years of experience, this multinational technology company specializes in retail, technology, and e-commerce. Alibaba provides customer-to-customer, business-to-business, and business-to-customer sales services with online portals and electronic payment options. You can search through the website by industry and find a factory that matches your needs.

MFG https://www.mfg.com/

MFG.com is the world's largest custom manufacturing marketplace that simplifies the process of locating a factory by offering a detailed database of manufacturing facilities both in the United States and overseas. Their website allows you to request and compare quotes and lead times, as well as track the progress of your order.

What to Look for in a Factory

Knowledge and Experience

You want to work with a factory that has proved their knowledge and experience. They should be able to answer all of your questions and confidently guide you through the process. If you've invented a food or beverage product, can the factory recommend a high-quality food chemist? Have a list of questions that you want to ask the factories you're considering, even simple ones that you know the answers to so you can test their knowledge.

Technical Capabilities

When searching for the right factory, you should only consider plants that produce products that are similar to your invention. Using a factory that makes the same goods you're looking to sell will ensure that they know and understand your market and what it will take to be successful.

Reputation

Once again, it comes down to reputation. What past and current customers have to say matters, and if anyone has experienced dirty dealings from a factory, you should consider the weight of their words. What other types of companies does the factory work with? Does the manufacturer have any regulatory fines or infractions that it's had to sort out? If the factory is overseas, what are its labor policies? It's crucial to find a manufacturer you trust.

Knowing What Questions to Ask

You should look for a factory that doesn't just have the tools you need to get the best product, but that also functions as a partner to purposely help you make an awesome product. A great factory is going to help your business in many other aspects of the production process, not just making parts and assembling your invention. To help you distinguish the good plants from the bad ones, here is a list of questions to ask during the vetting process.

- What experience do you have in this industry?

- Can you provide proof of recent inspections and audits?

- Who are your current clients?

- What are your minimum and maximum order requirements?

- What is the projected turnaround time for producing "X quantity" of my product?

- Is all of your work done in-house, or do you outsource to other facilities?

- Are all of your materials created in-house, or do you outsource the production of materials?

- Can you take care of the sourcing of materials or do I have to provide my own materials?

Finding Investors for Your Invention

Believe it or not, finding investors is one of the easier parts of getting funding for your invention. In fact, you have the potential of meeting with upwards of forty investors throughout this process, depending on your invention's niche and where you live. However, just as important as a quality idea and solid pitch to be successful, is finding a quality investor to back the production of your invention.

You need to find someone who ideally works in the same industry that your idea will be making its mark in. Being backed by an investor who comes from the same field as your invention will give you access to invaluable wisdom, and will probably be the best route in securing a financial agreement that is fair.

Unfortunately, we all don't get a chance at pitching top industry leaders on Shark Tank. So, while demonstrating how amazing your invention is to Mark Cuban, Barbara Corcoran, and the "Mr. Wonderful" Kevin O'Leary may be your biggest fantasy right now, it's best to look for more realistic ways for getting funding. When you are ready to pursue outside funding for your invention or business, consider these methods of finding angel investors and ways to locate venture capitalists.

Finding Angel Investors

1. Look into top-tier business schools in your area.

I know that we all don't have access to the very best business schools in the country. But, so you can still get the best industry knowledge and solid funding for your idea by looking in your own backyard. Once again, it comes down to research. Compare the statistics of the strongest business schools and entrepreneurial programs in your area and call the schools with any questions you have about their staff, alumni, and guest speakers. Universities generally have a solid and reliable network full of successful industry leaders, and they are usually open when providing resources.

2. Use your own network.

It doesn't matter if you are living in rural Pennsylvania or a metropolis in California, there are plenty of business owners and founders of companies close to home that can offer their advice and recommendations. Many investors specialize in specific markets, like retail, travel, or technology, and typically prefer to find additional companies to work with in their own network. One of the best things you can do as an entrepreneur is secure a place for yourself within one of those networks, and then do your own research on the angel investors you find within your field. Go to as many networking events as you can, join discussion groups on social media, and work to get an introduction with the investors you hope to work with.

3. Look no further than your own computer.

Many business owners and top-tier executives can be found online on websites like LinkedIn, AngelList, Quora, and MicroVentures. Take your time building your own credibility and online profiles on these sites so that when you reach out to angel investors, they have a clear snapshot of who you are and how your invention can make a great impact. Many of these platforms even have filters that allow you to view investors that are specifically in your own market.

Tips for Securing Funding

Put the Fun in Crowdfunding

Crowdfunding is the process of funding a project or enterprise by raising small amounts of money from many people, generally conducted through the internet. You've probably heard of a dozen success stories about people who have used the website GoFundMe to pay their way through school, fund movie ventures, and keep their businesses afloat. Unfortunately, it's not always that simple or easy to get your invention to market.

There are many crowdfunding platforms available that target specific industries, such as science, the arts, startups, etc. While you won't receive the same hands-on guidance as you would with an angel investor, you will still have a network of people who have some experience in your industry. Using online crowdfunding resources will require good social media skills and consistent customer outreach.

Gain a Reputation

Get recognition before asking for money. If you think your invention is good enough to pitch, then you should have already started fueling your reputation. You don't have to be rich to gain publicity, especially when you have so many online resources available. Work on building your social media presence and selling a limited stock of your invention. Go over your business model and associated numbers and make certain that you can defend your business choices and vision. You want to reduce any risk associated with investing in your idea to improve your chances of gaining an investor.

Utilize Accelerators

Apply to accelerator programs offered by investment firms, universities, and seed funds. These resources are available throughout most of North America and are relatively competitive. While it may be a difficult process with bigger entities like Techstars and YCombinator, the payoff can be huge. Accelerator programs are great opportunities to meet company founders, attend boot-camps that teach you how to launch a product and work with established entrepreneurs. Most accelerator programs culminate in a Demo Day presentation and pitch to an audience of real potential investors.

Chapter 4: Building Brands & Following Trends

As you have probably guessed, this next chapter is about building a brand for your product and predicting or following consumer and industry trends. If you're not looking to start a business and simply want to sell your invention, then you might be wondering why you shouldn't just skip this chapter. Aside from being filled with awesome and useful information, the importance of branding is highly misunderstood by those who are new to the business world.

Everything you see on social media speaks to an individual's brand or company's brand identity. Branding isn't just the logo of a company, it is a statement about what the company's values are and how it shows itself to the world. Branding your invention or service is crucial in standing out amongst all the other startups and innovators out there. It defines your product or service and makes it unique and recognizable to anyone who sees your media content and any products you may create later on.

What is a brand?

A brand is more than just a name or a color scheme. It is how other people perceive you and your products whenever they interact with your company. Even people, especially celebrities, work hard to have strong brands. Think of Kim

Kardashian - the color filters she uses on her photos, the backgrounds of her pictures, her clothing choices, hairstyles, makeup, charities she supports, and causes she advocates for.

For those who follow her on social media, it is easy to recognize a project she is involved in or products she has created simply because her brand is so strong that consumers instinctively know that she is the face behind it. And unless you have been living under a rock for the last decade, we all know just how rich and influential the Kardashians are in media and pop culture.

Now, you may not want to be the next Kim Kardashian by any means, but you can somewhat understand how and why branding is important. The question is, what do you want your brand to say about you and your product or service?

Exercise 1: Take a moment and think about your brand. We all have a name, a face, mannerisms, our own style, and different ways of communicating, all creating a lasting impact on who we are to different people we meet. Write down your name and five keywords that you would associate with your own personal brand.

Next, write down a few sentences about how you think you leave an impression on new people and whether they would describe you with those words. If not, what words would they use to describe you?

Now that you understand branding in terms of individuals, shift your focus to branding in the business world. Companies have names, logos, fonts, reputations, products, and logos that all work cohesively to make up how that business is seen in the eyes of consumers and competitors. But, you can't build a brand if any of these small things change.

Sure, you may want to mix up social media captions and the color choices of your product design. But the fact of the matter is that you cannot build a brand without being consistent.

You need to maintain consistency in your brand in every aspect as you expand and develop your business. You can't build a brand or be consistent without first establishing what your brand is. And, it essentially comes down to seven steps.

The 7 Steps of Establishing a Brand Identity

1. Research

Research your target audience, as well as your competitors. You've already done this in the beginning stages of developing your invention and prototype.

Exercise 2: You need to understand your customers and what the competition stands for and delivers to them without you entering the market. Answer these two questions: What does your competition's brand stand for? What does it say to your customers about their values?

Additionally, you need to define the following:

a. Who your "lowest hanging fruit" consumers are. These are the customers that you know will be the easiest to sell to.

b. Who your top competitors are. Don't ever think that your invention can't make it big time. Yes, there may be other brands on the market that have a strong presence, but your product is here for a reason and can fulfill your customer's needs better. Who is your competition and what do they bring to the table?

2. Choose your focus.

Decisively pick your focus and personality.

What does your invention say? Is it a solution to a serious problem? Does it provide a way to pass the time while having fun? Think deeply about the need that your product fills.

For example, most millennial women have a solid skincare routine and are willing to spend the money on quality products to ensure they are pampering themselves and nourishing their skin. But, the first step of creating a morning skincare routine is getting into the habit of washing your face. Most people don't think about this when they first wake up, so beauty and cosmetic companies need to use advertisements to get their target audience thinking about their products. The result? Commercials of young women and teenagers excitedly washing their faces with colorful products and showing off their glowing, clear skin after using the products.

These bath and body companies use fun and excitement to turn a chore into an experience. Of course, young women will buy the products; they make washing your face look enjoyable, and the best way to start off your day! Now, the question is, what is your invention's focus and personality?

Exercise 3: Write down five words that describe your invention, and five words that describe how you feel using it, or how you feel when it has solved your problem. The next step will require a little more creativity. Using at least two words from both prompts, create a personality for your product as if it was an actual person.

For example, if I were selling knitted socks, I would personify them as "a twenty to thirty-year-old woman who enjoys feeling comfortable, warm, and safe, who also likes reading, showing off her unique sense of style, and likes anything with a homemade touch."

3. Choose a name.

Choose your business/product/service name.

This may already be a no-brainer to you, but as someone who struggled for months trying to find the best product name, I definitely needed help with this step. After all, your invention's name has to make it stand out among your competitors, encompass everything your invention does and stands for, and speak to the function or purpose of your product.

The name of your product or business will affect your logo, marketing strategy, and web presence. You want a name that can't be confused with another product on the market and can be used to influence other product lines you might offer later on. If you are anything like me, then you might need a little help in the naming department. There are always business name generators available online -or you can try following one of the following approaches.

- Make up a word. Some examples include Häagen-Dazs, Pepsi, Xerox, Kodak, Sony, Google, and Ikea.

- Reframe the definition of an unrelated word. Examples of this technique are BlackBerry phones, Apple computers, Amazon -the largest online marketplace in the world, and Virgin media.

- Use a metaphor or suggestive word. Good examples are The Midas Touch, Kayak, Jaguar, Monsters, Twitter, and Nike.

- Use a word that describes exactly what your product is. For example, Windbreaker, Jet Ski, Wite-Out, Super Glue, and The Shoe Company.

- Create a name by altering a word or using Latin endings. See the examples of Tumblr, Jell-O, Ziploc, Panera Bread, Activia, and Soylent.

- Use the initials of a longer brand name or an acronym such as CVS, K-Mart, AT & T, HBO, H&M, A&W Root Beer, GEICO, and P.F. Chang's.

- Combine words together that describe your product in a concise way like Facebook, AutoZone, LinkedIn, WordPress, Comcast, Wal-Mart, Groupon, and Pinterest.

Keep in mind that your brand name will directly affect the URL of your product's website. So, make sure that you shop around with different names and ideas before settling on one. Also, it's best to run your name by several people and focus groups to see their reactions and whether the name has an unintended meaning or similarity to another product you might not have thought of.

4. Choose a catchphrase.

Write your slogan.

A catchy slogan is a good asset to have. It's a short and descriptive phrase that you can use in your advertising, packaging, business cards, and social media bio. A slogan with a punch can make a big impact with just a few words. A slogan is a short and memorable phrase used in advertising, religious organizations, political campaigns, and other contexts to express an idea or purpose with the intention of persuading a target audience. It's believed that it takes almost seven seconds to form a first impression, which is why slogans are so short.

Unlike a name, a slogan can be changed several times through your business's or product's development. Pepsi has changed its slogan over thirty times in the last few decades. When coming up with potential slogans, use these guidelines for inspiration:

- **State your claim.** Examples: "Melts in your mouth, not in your hand" -M&M's, "The Quicker Picker Upper" -Bounty, "The World's Strongest Coffee" -Death Wish Coffee.

- **Use a metaphor.** Examples: "Your daily ray of sunshine" -Tropicana, "So easy, a caveman could do it" -Geico, "Redbull gives you wings" -Redbull, "Taste the rainbow" -Skittles.

- **Reflect your customer's attitude.** Examples: "Because you're worth it" -L'oreal, "Just do it" -Nike, "Get in the zone" -AutoZone.

- **Write a rhyme.** Examples: "Beanz Meanz" -Heinz, "Do you... Yahoo!?" -Yahoo, "No battery is stronger longer" -Duracell, "The best part of waking up is Folgers in your cup" -Folgers.

5. Choose your colors and fonts.

The colors and fonts you choose for your product and packaging will visually represent your invention. They will also play an important role when you start building the website for your invention. Colors have a greater impact than you may realize. Even just looking at a color combination can spark a memory of your favorite toy or restaurant.

Like yellow and red, when put next to each other, you immediately think of McDonald's. Or that blue circle with a white 'F' on the inside that lets you know you've logged into Facebook. The colors of your brand convey the feeling you want to communicate to your customers and should be consistent across your brand and future products.

Color psychology isn't an exact science, but it can influence your choices. To help you choose the colors of your logos and fonts, here is a breakdown of emotions that are associated with specific colors.

- Red - Excitement, action, strength, passion, desire, energy, love, active, physical, bold, leader, willpower.

- Orange - Confidence, optimistic, success, uplifting, bravery, fun, sociability

- Yellow - Youth, positivity, caution, warmth, enthusiasm, creativity, playfulness, cheer, happiness, curiosity, cowardice, joy.

- **Green** - Nature, clarity, balance, positivity, quality, sanctuary, reassurance, freshness, generous, healing, growth, restore.

- **Blue** - Trust, authority, loyalty, intelligence, peace, serenity, communication, awareness, open, determination, perspective, content.

- **Purple** - Royalty, luxury, individuality, ambition, spirituality.

- **Pink** - Sweet, love, intuition, compassion, caring, assertive, sincerity, sensitive, nurture, feminine, floral, romantic.

- **Brown** - Serious, simple, richness, dependable, utility, rugged, subtle, natural.

- **Black** - Dramatic, classic, sophistication, distinctive, conservative, modern, security, formality, mystery, tradition.

- White - Simplistic, refined, clean, honesty, innocence, sterile, surrender, purity.

Now it's time to choose your fonts. At this point, the fonts that you use for your packaging and marketing are also most likely going to be the fonts you use on your website.

Not many consumers realize that a brand typically features two different fonts: one for the headings and another for the body text. The font for your logo can be different from the fonts you use for your website and advertisements.

Obviously, I can't write out every font in the universe to help you choose the perfect lettering for your invention. But, there are dozens of websites that will generate font pairings, as well as potential logos to help spark your creativity and choose the pairing that's right for your product.

6. Design your logo.

We touched on logos a little bit in the last chapter, but really only covered the legal rights in presenting a logo with your brand. Right now, we are going to focus more on the artistic and creative design that comes with creating a logo for your invention. A business logo is probably the first thing that comes to mind when you think about branding. And you're not wrong. A logo is the face of a company and represents the company everywhere that your brand and invention exists.

Just like your invention, you want a logo that is unique, identifiable among your competitors, and one store shelves, and that will be scalable in all sizes. This is a factor that is often overlooked but is important because you might want to produce packaging in varying sizes. Therefore, you should consider all the places where your brand's logo could possibly exist, from your website to your social media profile pictures.

Unlike colors and your target audience, you may have no idea which direction you want to take your logo in. There are several paths that you can take, and I have no doubt that you will find a design that makes sense for your brand. Here are a few design structures and examples that can help you get started.

- **Abstract Design.** An abstract design doesn't have an exact meaning. To put it simply, it could be a shape and colors that aren't easily correlated to anything else in the real world. It doesn't have an innate meaning and is completely unique. Examples: Google Chrome, Chase Bank, Pepsi, Gucci, Chanel, Reebok.

- **Mascot Design.** Mascots are one of the most popular advertising strategies and can be found amongst the most popular brands that are recognizable today. They are usually represented by the face of a character, and serve the purpose of humanizing your brand. However, it should be noted that many design and branding experts agree that mascot logos appear to be outdated in comparison to today's modern and minimalistic designs. Therefore, it's recommended that you only use a mascot logo in certain contexts, such as deliberately going for a retro design. Examples: Wendy by Wendy's Restaurant, Chester Cheetah by Cheetos.

- **Emblem Design.** Emblem designs are becoming increasingly popular, as the right design can be memorable, modern, and classic all at the same time. Emblems are typically circular and incorporate both text and a picture to create a sophisticated and bold look. Yet, if the design is overcomplicated, it could lose its impact, especially when shrunk down to fit on smaller spaces. Examples: Starbucks, Harley Davidson, Warner Brothers, General Electric, Stella Artois, and Harvard University.

- **Letter mark Design.** The letter mark (also referred to as a monogram) design is another classic logo choice that is easily recognizable by customers. A letter mark is often used by companies whose name has three or more words, incorporating the full business name into the logo design without taking up too much space. By using just a few letters, a company can effectively streamline its brand and strengthen its identity. Isn't it easier to say "NASA" than National Aeronautics and Space Administration? The focus should be on the initials of your invention or business, so the font you choose should reflect your brand and what the product or business does. It should also be clear and legible so customers can read it on your website and business cards. Examples: HBO (Home Box Office), LV (Louis Vuitton), CN (Cartoon Network), IBM (International Business Machines Corporation).

- **Icon Design.** The icon logo (also known as pictorial) design has become increasingly popular because of its minimalistic metaphorical approach. Unlike abstract designs, icon logos are suggestive about the product's function or purpose. For example, Twitter uses a small blue bird to represent its company, reflective of the "tweets" shared on its platform. However, as a new and unestablished brand, it's recommended that you don't use an icon logo by itself. Instead, you should incorporate your invention's name into the design to pair a letter mark or wordmark with the icon. Examples: Snapchat, Target, Apple, Shell, Playboy, Nike, Puma, Android, Windows Microsoft, YouTube, WhatsApp, Instagram.

- **Wordmark Design.** Commonly mistaken for letter mark, wordmark logos take your brand name, font, and color scheme and turn them into a cohesive visual representation of your brand's identity. The greatest challenge of having a wordmark design is, once again, legibility when shrunken down. However, using a wordmark design also allows you to incorporate an icon logo to accompany it, similar to how Facebook will also use the letter F in the blue circle, having two logos that can be used interchangeably. Wordmark logos are simple, yet playful in the coloring, spacing, and font, often used by the most notable brands you know today. Wordmarks can be used across many different media platforms, which is why they are so widely used. Of course, it all comes down to using the right typeface so that your invention's or company's name is legible and communicates the personality of your brand. Examples: Skype, eBay, Google, Groupon, Calvin Klein, Coca-Cola, Vans, The New York Times, Cannon, Oracle, Forbes, Disney, Kellogg's.

- **Combination Design.** As mentioned in the icon logo's description, you can combine two logo concepts to create one stand-alone design. You don't have to choose a wordmark over an icon when you can have the best of both worlds. Your brand name can stand front and center, while still having the option of featuring the icon when needed. From an artistic standpoint, you can play with the layout of the logo, different fonts, and colors before settling on the mark that best fits your brand's personality. Then, it doesn't matter if you use just the icon or mascot, or the letter mark or wordmark, your customers will be able to recognize your products regardless of which design you choose to incorporate. Examples: McDonald's, Burger King, Doritos, Master Card Amazon, Adidas, Bluetooth, Domino's Pizza, Rolex, Dove, Taco Bell, Intel, PBS, Walmart, Airbnb.

7. Apply, evolve, and grow.

Branding doesn't stop when you have settled on a logo or created your slogan. A brand should be consistent, but it should also grow and evolve as the market and world change. How many people would continue using Google if their design and brand were the same as it was twenty years ago? Every day, companies and celebrities are evolving their brand to fit their political agendas, meet the needs of younger and older audiences, and maintain relevance as our attention spans shorten.

While your packaging and identity should stay the same during the first few years of marketing and development, you should continue to shape and evolve your brand as you grow. The bigger your product or service gets, the bigger your audience will be. Your brand identity will have to meet the demands of your new customers and learn who those customers are and how your invention speaks to them.

While it is impossible to control how your brand is perceived by 100% of the population, you can influence customers in the right direction, make a good first impression, and manage your brand's reputation. Just put your best foot forward every chance you get and stay true to your core audience.

Marketing Your Product

Product marketing is one of the most crucial parts of any company's awareness initiative. Marketing is the study and management of business-consumer exchange relationships. It helps you gather information about your target audience, such as: identifying your customers, anticipating, and fulfilling your audience's wants and needs. One of the primary purposes of marketing is to attract new customers to your product. Without a solid and active marketing strategy, your invention will never achieve its maximum potential. The other goals of marketing are:

- Understanding your target audience better.

- Targeting your buyer personas more efficiently. A buyer persona is a semi-fictional depiction of your ideal customer based on market research and data gathered about your current customers.

- Learning more about your competitors, their products, and advertising methods.

- To make certain that your product, sales, and marketing teams/strategies are all on the same page.

- To boost revenue and increase sales.

Unless you hire a marketing team or a marketing VP, then you are solely in charge of making sure that you are doing everything possible to market your invention correctly and effectively. As the product marketer, you have to ask yourself important questions about your product, such as:

- Is my invention relevant and applicable to today's market?

- Is my invention suitable for my target customers today?

- How is my invention unique from similar products on the market?

- Is there a better way to differentiate my invention from those of my competitors?

Product marketing compels you to look at your invention from a strategic point of view to ensure that it is successful among consumers in the present market. As the marketing manager, you will have specific responsibilities, such as creating content, managing resources, and maintaining a budget. As your business grows, you may need to invest in a team whose only priority is product marketing. Before we get into the details of marketing various strategies, you first need to understand the fundamentals of product marketing vs. conventional marketing.

Product Marketing vs. Conventional Marketing

Product marketing is much more strategic, whereas conventional marketing is exhaustive in its reach. Product marketing is thought to be an extension of conventional marketing. However, product marketing is regarded as possibly the most important component of a company's marketing efforts. Product marketing focuses on driving the demand for a product among your pre-existing customers. Its attention is focused on the steps consumers will take to buy your invention so that you or your marketing team can create campaigns to support the evidence gathered during the research and trial phases.

Product marketing comes down to understanding your invention's audience on a deep level and developing your invention's position in the market and the messaging used to appeal to your target customer base. Product marketing covers the launching of a product, as well as the execution of the entire marketing strategy. This is why the marketing teams at high-level companies are so highly regarded compared to the sales and product teams.

Conventional marketing, on the other hand, is focused on topics that fall underneath the umbrella of marketing. For example, the team researches and conducts lead generation, search engine optimization (SEO), and anything that relates to gaining new customers and converting leads into sales. The conventional marketing team works to promote the business and brand as a whole, which will include any products that are sold by the company. Hence why product marketing is an extension of conventional marketing. The core of the marketing team ensures that all of the content produced is on-brand and consistent.

Competitive Pricing vs. Value-Based Product Pricing

Pricing is something you may or may not have already thought about. If your invention is one of a kind, then it may be difficult to place a reasonable price on it. Or maybe you were going to seek the advice of a practiced industry leader before settling on a price. Regardless, there are two routes you can take when coming up with the right price for your invention. The first is competitive pricing.

Competitive pricing means that you are establishing your invention's price off of similar products sold by your competitors. This is the ideal method of pricing for businesses or individuals who have created a product similar to several others on the market. For example, a new type of super absorbent paper towels or an advanced garbage bag that holds ten times the weight of any other brand out there. If you believe that your invention is unique enough to warrant a noticeably higher price than all of the options offered by your competitors, then you have found solid data to back up your pricing decision. The best way to establish competitive pricing is to evaluate the fairness of your competitor's prices, as well as their financial reports and industry trends within the market.

On the other side of the coin lies value-based pricing. Value-based pricing gives you the opportunity to maximize your profit; however, it can be time-consuming when it comes to demonstrating its superiority over your competitor's prices and products. This method of finding the perfect price for your product is ideal for markets with very few competitors, and even more so for inventions that are entirely new and have unique features. Value-based pricing legitimizes your invention's value in a way that your customers can relate to their advantages. Your invention's price point is based on how much your customer will value it, rather than what the market, industry, or competitors say.

4 Tips for Successful Marketing

1. Tell a Story with Your Product

This is one of the most common marketing strategies out there, just ask any copywriter! Too many marketers and advertisers get caught up in the mindset of selling the product, not the experience. But to be honest, no one wants your invention. No one wants to buy any product, period. What they want is a solution to their problem. But, you have to show them why your invention is like nothing they've ever seen before.

If you only talk about the advantages, facts, and features of your invention, then you are leaving giant holes in your strategy where you could be getting and utilizing direct customer engagement. When you talk strictly about the facts, figures, and benefits, your customer's brain is simply working to decode the meaning of your words while remaining disconnected from your message.

But, if you tell a story, everything changes. Telling a true story about your invention, featuring a character that elicits intense emotions, engages larger portions of the brain. This is a prime example of how our emotions influence our decisions to buy. Storytelling is the easiest and most effective way to communicate your invention's value in a way that is memorable.

2. Don't Work Against Your Brand's Perception

This is where many marketing campaigns fail miserably. You've probably witnessed this story too many times to count. Big companies go so far outside of their market's perception that they completely miss the mark with their product.

For example, remember Google Glasses? What many experts thought would be the future of technology and fashion was quickly thrown to the wayside. The techwear was too expensive for most people, and issues of privacy and the cultural backlash caused a disconnect between customers and Google's brand identity.

A few other examples worth mentioning are Life Savers soda, which did well in taste tests but made customers think they were drinking liquid candy. Nike's Fuel Band, a fitness tracker that tested the company's tech department, yet couldn't measure up to its competitors, the Fitbit and the Apple Watch. And last but not least, Bic's disposable underpants and tights. Turns out their customers favored their lighters, razors, and pens over their disposable undies.

3. Do What Your Competition Won't - Challenge the Status Quo

When Nike first came into the marketplace, they exploded with growth. Mostly due to their fearless innovation to try things their competitors simply wouldn't do. They failed many times and in big ways. But, they finally hit the nail on the head when they used an untapped and even criticized marketing tactic: celebrity endorsements. This seems unimaginable now when even small-fish social media "influencers" will sell anything for a commission. But, for the emerging Nike, this made their name unforgettable since the early 1970s.

By 1980, their unique marketing strategy had grown the company's revenue to nearly three million dollars. With the signing of Michael Jordan as their celebrity face, Nike's value hit over two billion dollars by 1990. It just goes to show that new tricks are underrated and that you should never be afraid of being different.

4. Fail Fast, Fail Often, and Move Forward

This is a phrase that many seasoned businessmen and entrepreneurs live by. It's how most of them got their start to begin with. There is no industry that guarantees you a job or success -especially when it comes to something as fluid as product invention. You are going to fail, probably more times than you can count -and that's okay! It's what you're supposed to do. Failing with a marketing campaign or second prototype of your product will get you that much closer to unbelievable success. Of course, there are ways that you side-step obvious red flags.

For example, trying to find a market for your invention before you know that a market exists is almost certain to bring you failure. Many inventors believe so much in their product that it's the best thing to be introduced to humanity, that they never check with the market.

A prime example of this is when inventor Dean Kame was rumored to have created the greatest alternative to the automobile. He predicted selling at least ten thousand electric scooters a week at the price tag of five thousand dollars. Unfortunately, customers and investors hated the electric scooter, and Kamen only sold twenty-four thousand units in five years. Yikes.

Fortunately for Kamen, his net worth stands at about five hundred million dollars. Regardless of his monumental national failure, Kamen continued to create and sell many of his inventions, like the Segway and has a promising future in innovative technology.

Digital Marketing

You have probably been wondering when we would get to this point. Digital marketing is possibly the most revolutionary method of selling since television ads. You see it every time you pick up your cell phone, turn on your computer, open up your email. It is a beast in and of itself that grows increasingly more complicated as society becomes more involved in the virtual world. But, if you don't start trying to understand it now, you never will. Thankfully, there are experts who have studied, practiced, and researched the ins and outs of internet marketing and shared their findings with us.

To be honest, digital marketing isn't as difficult as you may think. When looking at the internet as a whole and the many platforms you can use, it's easy to get overwhelmed by the possibilities and algorithms. But, if you look at each outlet individually, then digital marketing actually becomes easy and fun. For example, Twitter, Facebook, Instagram, and Snapchat are the peak of internet marketing campaigns. They are all flooded with content and your competitors. However, they each function differently, and when broken down, their backends are easy to maneuver and use to your advantage.

Digital Marketing Basics

Let's not get ahead of ourselves, though. First, let's get down to the basics. "What is digital marketing?" Digital marketing is the action of selling and advertising products and services by using online marketing tactics to your advantage, such as social media marketing, email marketing, and search marketing. At its core, digital marketing is simply marketing done on the internet.

Today, it is the most efficient way businesses are getting their message out to their best prospects and audience. Marketing is the right to make an offer and the right time and in the right place. Only now, your target audience is online, using social media, staying updated on world news with websites and blogs, and using search engines to find what they need. Internet marketing puts your company in the same channels as your customers, so that the best prospects are exposed visually to you, can learn more about your products, and even reach out directly with any questions they may have.

If you are new to internet marketing, it's important to learn the different tactics that work together to create a solid foundation for your product's marketing campaign. Regardless of which platform you use to market your product, digital media marketing comes down to attracting prospective customers, nurturing the relationships you create, and making offers that your audience will value and respond to.

How Does Internet Marketing Work?

In many ways, internet marketing is very similar to conventional marketing. Smart businesses seek to build mutually beneficial relationships with customers and leads. However, for the most part, internet marketing has replaced conventional tactics because it is simply the best way to reach today's consumers.

For example, what was the last big purchase you made? Perhaps it was a new phone, hiring a utility worker to fix something in your home, or even purchasing a new home. Regardless of what it was, you most likely began your search by looking online for solutions, the best provider, and what the best options were based on your budget. The reviews you read online probably influenced your decision, as well as any comments you may have received on your social media accounts and the pricing options that you found on various websites.

The fact of the matter is that most big purchase decisions start on the internet. This being the way the world works now, an online presence is necessary for any business or new product. Anyone else who thinks differently is surely going to fall behind the times and will eventually see their customer base dwindle as more shoppers convert to online buyers.

The good news is that it doesn't matter what your invention is, you can sell almost anything online.

The solution to creating a strong impact with your product is to develop an online marketing plan that puts your invention on all the platforms your followers are already spending the majority of their time on. Then, using various channels to connect them in different ways.

For example, you would use helpful and intelligent content to keep your customers in the know with industry news, the issues they're facing, and how you are able to solve those issues. Then, you would use social media, like Instagram, Twitter, Facebook, etc. to share the content you create and engage with your customers and followers as a friend. Like how Pizza Hut, Wendy's, and other large chains actively engage their followers in the comments sections of their posts and talk to them like they already have a relationship.

You would also use search engine optimization to optimize your articles and postings. When done correctly, your content will appear above your competitors' whenever a potential customer is searching for the information you've already written about.

The next step is to use advertising to drive traffic to your social media pages and websites so that potential customers and leads can see your offers. There are other tactics you can use along the way that will help direct traffic and produce more sales, like email marketing and video campaigns. When all of these pieces are put together, you have an efficient but simple internet marketing set up.

Digital Marketing Strategy Guide

I know I just threw a lot of information at you. And while it looks intimidating on paper, building that functioning marketing machine from the ground up can be quick and easy. That is why I've included a short guide in this chapter to help you create and perfect a digital marketing strategy without the confusion and missteps that come with trying to do it alone.

Utilizing Smartphones

When they first appeared nearly twenty years ago, smartphones were clearly the direction of the future. And while the first models in 1992 didn't have even a fraction of the functions today's cell phones do, they were the beginning of a new era of consumerism and technology.

Today, more than eighty percent of web users own a smartphone. We officially crossed the tipping point of more users accessing the internet from their phones than their computers in 2014. This brings us to the first type of digital marketing: mobile marketing. More money is spent on mobile advertisements than desktop advertisements and possibly even TV ads.

Over fifty percent of consumers prefer to buy from businesses that promote their products via the internet. The United States alone is expected to have three hundred million online shoppers in the year 2023 -over ninety percent of the entire nation's population! This just goes to show that while your values may be traditional or you may prefer to go to the store to buy milk, the audience you're trying to convert to real sales is online. They want to buy online products, and you have the advantage of giving them the opportunity to fulfill their wants and needs.

Of course, with everyone logging onto the internet to make purchases, there are challenges that follow for business owners. The competition changed from the neighboring stores down the street to global competitors, making the selling game even more intense and international. Industry giants like Amazon are your biggest contenders, and you have to evaluate their marketing methods just as often as you do your own. This also means that you have to be willing to spend money to make money.

Finding the right method of digital advertising for your invention is the difference between paying unnecessary and unstable startup costs to get off the ground and making a real profit in the e-commerce space. The more coordinated and regulated your internet marking methods are, the greater your return on investment (ROI) you'll again, regardless of your competition. Now, let's move onto the best ways to promote your invention and services online, and which ones will benefit your sales goals the most.

Social Media Advertising

Electronically selling your products or services online and social media advertising go hand in hand. While membership numbers are slowly receding, Facebook can actually claim fifty-two percent of all online product sales. Even Pinterest advertisements are thirty percent more effective than other display ad tactics, like websites and phone apps. But, how effective social media marketing is for you depends on the product and brand you are selling and the audience you want to reach.

Facebook Ads

If you, like many other marketers, are considering using Facebook advertisements to promote your product or service, here is everything you need to know.

On average, a Facebook cost-per-click (CPC) is approximately forty cents. This means that you can advertise your inventions on Facebook for at little as ten dollars a day and still achieve a decent conversion rate. Of course, your costs will increase depending on certain determinants. But, if you understand them well enough, you can get the most out of Facebook ads.

The first factor to consider is that your cost-per-click might be higher in other countries that you sell your product in. For example, the CPC for Japan in 2016 was about seventy-three cents, while in Greece, it went as low as seventeen cents. This is data that you can gather and track by yourself as you begin using Facebook ads.

The second factor that comes into play is the time of year. This is a rule of thumb that started with conventional marketing, and you see it everywhere you go. Just think about how many commercials and advertisements you see around the holidays of Christmas, Valentine's Day, Easter. When tapping into the seasonal market, your costs will undoubtedly be higher. In general, you will spend much more money on social media advertisements between the months of October and December.

Third, the costs of your advertisements are also impacted by the age groups you target in individual ads. This is a simple feature that has made new age marketing even more user-friendly. While the most active users online are millennials and Generation Z, targeting users between the ages of 45 to 65 will cost more. This is because this age group makes more money and is more likely to spend it.

The fourth factor to take into account is the timing of your advertisements. Advertising costs will increase in the early morning hours because that is the time when most people are logging into Facebook for updates before going into work. The cost will then rise again in the evening, after standard work hours when everyone is one their way home or already relaxing on the couch.

What many Facebook marketers don't know is that the cost of your product and the time that you can sell it during the day will depend on the type of product or service you are selling. Some products have a usual time slot. For example, most people will start thinking about what they will have for dinner in the late afternoon. Therefore, time-sensitive ads are most likely to get traffic even though they will be much more expensive to run.

Not to mention the obvious, but it's worth noting, if you want your advertisements to appear at the top of the Facebook newsfeed, then you will have to pay more for that prime position. Last, but definitely not least, comes another retail truth.

You will pay more to advertise your product if your primary target audience is female. It is more competitive to reach women as more and more businesses are marketing to them. They spend more money online and on retail in general. So, it's not that surprising that you're going to have to pay more to market your invention to them.

When you start experimenting with Facebook ads, track the different characteristics that drive up your CPC's. Oftentimes, you will see that similar factors will increase the cost of your ads across different social media platforms. If you pay attention to the statistics provided by your analytic tools, then you can keep your advertising costs low while still increasing sales.

Facebook is the ideal marketplace for any conventional and legal product or service. With over one billion daily users, you have a wide range of interests and purchase behaviors to use to your advantage as an inventor. Unsurprisingly, the most clicks go to technology, retail, fitness, and beauty products. After all, they are the easiest businesses and products to market on the internet.

While you can sell almost anything on Facebook, there are limits. Their ad systems automatically prohibit advertisements for:

- Illegal drugs
- Drug paraphernalia
- Prescriptions
- Tobacco and tobacco-related products
- Firearms
- Animals
- Any pirated products or services that promote piracy
- Downloadable content

When you are creating content for your ads, it's been proven that using less than twenty percent of the ad space for text will result in better performance. After all, humans tend to be more visual and won't stop to read a detailed paragraph about why they should buy your product. They'll just see a block of words and continue scrolling. Ads that feature short bursts of information perform better across the board.

Remember that Facebook wants your boosted posts and advertisements to do well too. That's how they make money. So, if your ad gets blocked, rejected, or taken down, don't get discouraged. You're going to experience many trial and error phases as an inventor, and especially as a marketer. That's just how the industry works, the best copywriters, salesmen, and advertisers experiment and fail the most. The more you fail, the more you learn, the more knowledge you can apply to streamline your income.

Instagram Ads

Instagram was created in 2010. And in 2012, the platform was bought by Facebook. Therefore, Instagram advertisements actually work off of the Facebook algorithm. So, this section will be shorter than the prior since most of the information is the same. Let's get right down to the financials.

Even though Instagram is owned by Facebook, and the advertisement set up is similar, it costs more to run ads on Instagram. You may average a dollar and change for just one click, while on Facebook, you can buy clicks for less than half the price. And when it comes to selling in the U.S. marketplace, it isn't uncommon to pay close to four dollars for clicks in certain industries.

This means that if you choose to pay for cost per one thousand "impressions" on Instagram, it will average to about eight dollars. Even though many new businesses and product launchers work off a limited budget, the benefit of using Instagram is that paying for views will increase your product awareness faster. This means that sales take a backseat for the time being.

As of 2016, the average click-through -rate on Instagram was about .52%. While this statistic proves to be better than most other digital marketing methods, it is still a smaller percentage than Facebook. Consumers like to engage and buy on Facebook and Instagram.

However, if your product directly competes with a bigger brand, like Apple, then the cost of your clicks will go up. The key to successfully marketing on Instagram is using these facts to your advantage. Because the immediate goal isn't always to make sales -but to increase the awareness around your product and gain consumer popularity and familiarity.

For example, more than sixty percent of all e-commerce purchases are made on a smartphone. More consumers have an iPhone, making Apple the greatest stakeholder in customer buying behavior. It was also found that owning Apple products is the primary indicator of personal wealth. This means that even though you don't want to necessarily compete with Apple, you can target your ads to Apple users in anticipation of making more sales while still increasing brand awareness.

Instagram is quickly making headway for businesses and aspiring entrepreneurs, thanks mostly to the shoppable post feature that allows you to tag your actual products in the pictures you post. Social media marketing experts all agree that Instagram is the future of selling products and services online.

Unfortunately, this realm of online shopping is still new, and therefore prone to frequent development changes and updates to better fit the needs of businesses. For now, it's better to save time and money by complying with Facebook's store and product policies detailed previously in the chapter and see if your product falls under the top Instagram sales trends.

- Wireless headphones/earbuds

- Beauty and skincare products

- Ketogenic and Vegan products

- Affordable fashion-forward retail and clothing

- Sustainable fashion

- Sneakers

- Wigs and hair extensions

- Reusable bags and home decor items

Google Ads

Last, but not least, comes Google Search Ads. With the examples of Facebook and Instagram, it's clear that visual ads have the upper hand and that it's best to use very little (if any) text. But when it comes to Google, visual content is not always the way to go. As a matter of fact, visual ads are less impactful on Google, even though you have about fifteen to twenty words to make a statement and entice your customers.

Text-based advertisements are undoubtedly more expensive than visual ones. However, when done efficiently and effectively, text ads will prove to show higher conversion rates than your average social media ads. The return on investment is certainly there, but you can expect to pay for clicks that don't convert to sales in the beginning stages of Google ads. You can expect to pay approximately three dollars per click (sometimes even more) for when your text-based ad is selling well.

Google will track the progress of your ads and factor the data into your quality score. If you don't pay attention to your quality score, then you'll end up paying more to post your ads. While Facebook will slowly stop showing your ads to viewers, Google will continue showing it while making you pay unreasonable prices for clicks. If you do well and achieve a quality score of ten, Google will reward you with a thirty percent discount. However, letting your score plummet to one will result in Google charging you up to six hundred percent more than they charge your competition. This could mean paying up to eighteen dollars for just one click!

Your best strategy is to run a Google ad campaign and collect as much research as you can about what keywords to use, and who the competition is targeting with their ads. You should also be aware of language that could shine a negative light on your brand. Words like "free" and "discount" can result in a lower quality score, but so can other words that are directly associated with the market for your invention. You should research negative keywords that are specific to your product, market, industry, and target customers so that you can convert sales more efficiently and stand out among the competition.

4 Specific Tips for Getting the Most Out of Social Media Advertising

When you're a small business with an even smaller budget, you want to get the best bang for your buck - regardless of which platform you use. To maximize your results while still working within your budget, follow these quick tips.

1. Set a Budget

To work within a budget, you have to first establish a budget. The cost per click is not the only thing you are going to have to pay for -unless you're already a qualified marketing wizard. You need to hire someone to create your content and graphics, write your copy, and manage the ad campaign, among other things. I live by the belief that you should always assume there are going to be issues throughout the process and that you will spend more than you think.

Social media ads need constant maintenance and monitoring. Research your target demographic across platforms, run several ads based on your audience's preferences and interest, gather the data, revise, and repeat. Then, start setting a budget on what you're willing to spend on advertisements and on hiring people to help reach your marketing goals. Stick to that budget for a few weeks until you either outgrow it or need to revise it based on your ad performance.

2. Practice Relevancy

One little known secret about Instagram and Facebook is that they give your advertisements a relevance score. If your advertisements don't seem relevant to the users who view it, then they will charge you more for ads and show them less often. On average, a business will pay fifteen cents more per click, but get seventy-five fewer clicks when the platform considers it irrelevant.

The best strategy is to use Facebook's advertising tools to target a smaller but more on-brand audience that will enhance your statistics according to Facebook's algorithm. Not only does this tactic help you reach the right people with your ads, but it will also decrease the cost of misclicks (customers who saw your ad, but didn't click it). The end result? Making more online sales for less money.

3. Invest in the Visuals

Every day social media is becoming more and more visual. Instagram, Pinterest, and Snapchat are all geared towards sharing visual content like pictures and videos while sharing long statuses on Facebook is falling to the wayside. The reason? No one wants to spend two minutes reading a paragraph about a product. They will spend thirty seconds watching a short ad video that is engaging, colorful, and gets down to the benefits of your invention.

Products and services that are displayed through stunning visuals are more likely to be shared by your followers. You will get more clicks, increase your conversion rate, and make more sales. Use powerful imagery to evoke emotion from your views so they can resonate with your brand's message and share it with others.

4. Create Strong Landing Pages

A landing page is the web page where your lead can immediately purchase your product using an "add to cart" or "buy now" button. It is not the homepage to your website, nor is it a product category page. And with already investing in social media pages and a website, you might be wondering if you even need a landing page.

The answer is "yes," yes, you do. Facebook and Google factor your landing page into your relevance score and will push your ads to the top of the newsfeed based on how seamless your landing page is. If you take the time to create a seamless journey from the ad or your profile to your product's landing page, you will see a higher conversion rate, and you'll save money.

Chapter 5: Ready to Launch

Congratulations! You have finally made it to the launch of your new product! After months, maybe even years of hard work, headaches, and non-stop grinding, you are finally ready to showcase your invention to your audience. It's an exciting time, and you should take a moment to appreciate how much you have put into this product and how much it will change the lives of your customers.

The launch is one of the most important phases in creating and selling a brand new product or service. It introduces your invention to the world, and the response you get from your audience will dictate how the next few months will go, whether you find immediate success or have to go back to the drawing board. But first, let's get right into how to make your launch amazing.

Internal v. External: Launching Your Product

A product launch all comes down to marketing. And, as the sole product marketer, there are two main elements that you need to focus on: the internal launch (what goes on within your business while gearing up for your product launch) and the external launch (what is happening outside of your business with your customers and audience at the time of your product launch).

Internal Product Launch

Before the external product launch, you need to make sure that your entire team is on the same page. Your customers are going to rely on you and everyone in your organization to give accurate and consistent information about the product. Think of your employees and other team members as internal customers. If they are not on board with your product and the upcoming external launch, then it can greatly impact the success of your external launch.

Without complete knowledge and one hundred percent commitment to the product, they will not be capable of effectively communicating with prospective customers. Your internal resources are the backbone of your product or business. A successful external launch can only be achieved if your team is committed, especially if they are the ones who control the designing, marketing, selling, and distribution of the product. Therefore, internal communication is the key to overall success.

Here's a real example of how important an internal launch is. When I was in my early twenties, I worked at the front desk of a local gym. The owner was about to open his third location, and there was a lot of hype in the community surrounding it. However, both teams of employees at the current locations were at best excited, and at worst indifferent. While the marketing team spent all their energy on promoting the newest venue, most other employees knew very little about the gym and didn't even see the inside of it until it was opened to the public.

The result was confusion about launch dates, equipment details, amenities, parking, the list goes on. No one outside of the marketing team and company's VP's knew or even cared about the small details because they were excluded from the conversation. Whereas if the company spoke directly to their employees, there could've been a bigger external launch and a lot more support within the local community.

The driving purpose of an internal launch is to highlight the strategic benefits of the product and encourage a greater level of interest before the invention is introduced to the public. One of the most effective ways that you can ensure a strong internal launch is to get everyone in the company involved and make sure that they know the product inside and out. This can be done by creating a launch guide, a small booklet that answers, and potential questions your internal audience may have. Start by answering the following prompts.

1. Background Information

    a. What is the product or service?

    b. How does the product or service affect current and target customers?

    c. How will it attract customers outside of the targeted range?

    d. How does the product fit within the company's values?

2. Features and Benefits

    a. What are the features of the product or service?

b. What benefits does the product or service provide?

c. Is there additional training available for your team, so they understand how to use the product?

d. What support system can your team count on if they have more questions about the product or can't answer a customer's question?

3. External Launch Description

a. Explain the details of the launch and events that promote the launch.

b. Details of advertising initiatives and any current or upcoming promotions.

c. Levels of support available for each department.

4. Outline the Launch Schedule

   a. Training times and dates for team members to practice answering customer inquiries, solving problems, and providing helpful and direct customer service.

   b. Provide a detailed schedule of launch events and a timeline of goals or quotas.

   c. Provide a schedule of upcoming ad campaigns and awareness initiatives.

   d. Provide details to any customer events, expos, store opening, farmer's markets, anywhere you are featuring your product in a public space.

5 Ways to Hold a Successful External Product Launch

Now that you have the full support and understanding of your team, it's time to take your product to the public! There are many ways that you can market your product externally, as you already know from the last chapter. Your greatest asset for marketing is the internet, as it provides a large reach, a clear path to your target audience, and the ability to spread information and awareness fast. However, there are a few key tips that can take your external launch from "good enough" to "better than I could have ever imagined!"

1. Build the hype early.

Many new companies and startups make the common mistake of waiting until their product launches to start marketing it. If this is your timeline now, then you're already setting yourself up for failure. If you fail to start early, then you are already behind. One of the best ways to build hype early is by making the announcement of your product into a big deal.

Think of Apple and its keynote presentations. Apple has been using this tactic for years, and now its customers already decide to buy the product they are announcing just in anticipation of the event. Obviously, this strategy can be overreaching if you are a new business or a solo entrepreneur. What you can do is get your audience hooked on your invention before it's even released. Start building the hype a few weeks before your product is officially available.

That means posting on social media, being interactive in the comments section with followers, sharing visually stunning videos of your product at work, etc. The idea of building hype works best when your target customers already know the features and benefits of your product and have time to research it for themselves. Building hype before releasing your invention to the world will help generate immediate sales.

2. Take pre-orders sooner, rather than later.

When the gym that I worked at started marketing the newest facility, the marketing team did one thing absolutely right. They started selling memberships at a discount. This marketing move allowed the gym to start making a profit right away and helped with the rising construction costs. Once again, you want to start early before you fall behind. You don't need to wait until your invention is in stock before you generate sales. You can allow customers to pre-order your product so that you can start making a profit.

Pre-ordering doesn't just help you secure profit early, it also gives your customers a feeling of exclusivity. They will have something before anyone else has the chance to order it, being one of the first people to have your product in their hands. You can offer a discounted rate for the first one hundred customers, advertise a limited stock of supplies, or even include a free gift or free expedited shipping to help build the hype of pre-ordering. After all, if they don't order your product now, they may not have the chance to purchase it when it comes out on the official release date. Pre-ordering is another way to ensure that your invention gets a strong start right out of the gate.

3. Offer exclusive rewards to loyal clientele.

Going off the ending of the last point, one of the best ways to start building momentum early on in the pre-launch phase is by offering exclusive discounts and deals. After all, who doesn't love saving money and having exclusive access?

Depending on how you've constructed your brand image and pricing strategy, you can offer a discount for anyone who pre-order or to the people within your immediate social network. While it seems like everyone from your next-door neighbor to your cousin is selling something online in an attempt of network marketing, you'll be surprised how quickly your inner circle will jump to try out your new invention first.

This tactic becomes easier with each new product you create. But, if this is your first time creating a product or service, then you have to rely on the people you know to help boost your consumer awareness. With your social media marketing initiatives that you should have started early on and the familiarity of your invention within your circle of friends and family members, you already have existing clientele. These are the people you should contact first.

Believe it or not, most brands don't offer discounts for new products. Instead, when a new product comes along, they discount the prices of older merchandise to get rid of it. Offering a discount to your loyal clientele (the ones who have been on your social media since day one) lets them and newer followers know that you aren't going to give them another chance to save money.

If consumers know you're going to offer discounts later on, they will put off purchasing your product. Your product's discount should have urgency and only be offered for a limited time. Offering discounts and giveaways to customers that are already easy to reach will increase brand awareness.

4. Run a contest or giveaway.

I have personally never won a giveaway -not that I'm complaining! But, it was a cool and rewarding experience to offer that chance to someone else who really wanted my product. And getting client testimonials before I even debuted my invention was a valuable benefit. The first radio contest giveaway was in 1935, and stations, television networks, celebrities, and businesses of all sizes still use this tactic today because it's that efficient.

It may sound counterproductive (you want to make money, not lose it), but contests get people interested in your product, which could lead to more sales down the line. It hardly costs anything to run a contest -it can be entirely done on social media platforms, with the only expense being the cost of the product you're giving away (and shipping charges). Hosting a contest on social media exposes your invention to a bigger audience and builds excitement for your product, even by people who don't win.

5. Get the timing right.

Timing is everything. Your invention can be the greatest product of the year. But if you launch it at the wrong time, you could lose out on sales. For example, if you are planning to launch your product on a Friday that just happens to fall on July 3rd, then you are already starting off on the wrong foot.

July 4th is a national holiday that is celebrated by the entire United States, so most of the country will be shut down from that Friday until Monday morning for a long weekend. That means many people will be traveling, on vacation, spending time with friends and family, attending events, and basically not spending any time on their phones or on social media. They won't have any time or incentive to buy something online.

One strategy for choosing the perfect launch time and date is studying the analytics gathered by social media tools. You know that Facebook and Google can show you how many people are seeing your posts, the time of day your posts get the most interaction, and the days of the week most people are on social media. Use these numbers to your advantage on top of national and religious calendar events, and seasonal changes.

You can also do research on when your competition has released their previous products. For example, Apple always launches their smartphones in September, while Samsung releases their newest phones in the spring. Knowing your industry's trends and competitor's habits will help you determine the ideal time to introduce your product to the world.

Managing Your Inventory

Inventory management allows you to have your products in the right quantity for sale, and at the right time when it is needed. Without proper management, you can end up having too much or too little of your product and lose out on sales.

When done effectively, you can reduce the costs of storing excess while still maximizing sales. However, inventory management is not just about ordering and storing units of your product. It's about having the right amount on hand, avoiding waste, and avoiding the dreaded mistake of having too many products and not enough people buying it.

As a new business, you want to sell as many units of your invention as possible -without breaking the bank by ordering too much from your manufacturer. And if you are selling your invention out of your home as I did, then you don't have any time, space, or inventory to waste. To help you with the tough decisions of ordering and manufacturing, here are the best inventory practices for small enterprises.

Calibrate your forecasting.

Accurate forecasting is critical during the early stages of launching your product. Your projected sales calculations should factor in your competitors' past sales figures (which are often available online), the retail season cycle (pre-Christmas hype and summer trends are examples of this), market trends, changes in the economy, marketing efforts, etc.

Use the FIFO strategy (first in, first out).

This means that any products you sell should be in chronological order of when they were first purchased and created. This is especially vital for any perishable goods, like makeup or food products. If you were selling homemade chocolate, then you would sell the first batch you made before any other products -to ensure quality and freshness.

This approach should be practiced regardless of what you are selling. Following the FIFO method also creates the opportunity of bettering your organizational systems. You can label your products with a color-coding system that ensures employees are pulling the right products and shipping them to the correct customers.

Keep a close eye on the units that sell, and the ones that don't.

In an ideal world, you would continuously sell your invention in every size and color you have available and still have orders coming in every day.

Unfortunately, the world of business doesn't abide by our hopes and dreams. So, if you have products in several colors, sizes, or with different features, then it's important to identify low-turn stock. Low-turn stock are products that aren't selling well within the last few weeks or months, which means that you should stop stocking them.

Set up a system to routinely audit your inventory.

Regardless of whether you use inventory management software or not, as the owner of your invention, it is your responsibility to count your inventory to make sure your business is running smoothly. All too many times, you make the mistake of thinking there are more units than what you actually have, or products expire (if your product is related to food or health and beauty), and other small hiccups that throw your inventory off track. These issues can easily be solved and even avoided by personally counting your inventory at least once a week and seeing for yourself how much stock you are turning.

Think about investing in inventory management software.

I know that right now you're looking to cut costs and save money so that you can turn a profit faster. However, cloud-based inventory management software can provide real-time sales analytics, direct connection to your point of sale, and track your inventory as it moves. In the end, an investment like this could save you time and money.

Manage your assets as they wear down.

This may sound like a no-brainer, but everyone is guilty of waiting until an appliance is on its last leg before getting a new one. If you are manufacturing or packaging your invention in-house, then you need to make sure that your equipment and supplies are all fully operational and effective.

For example, if you are making graphic t-shirts and your printer is slowly dying, just make the investment of buying a new one instead of trying to make the old one last longer. A broken piece of machinery can cost you and your workers time and money, so do your best to monitor and replace your supplies as needed.

Never sacrifice quality.

Have you ever gone out to eat at your favorite restaurant, only to find that the owner needed to cut costs by buying lower quality ingredients? Suddenly the chicken is rubbery, the spinach is wilted, and you can tell that the condiments are from a knock-off brand. While the owner may have changed to a cheaper supplier to save money, now no one wants to eat at his restaurant because the quality has gone downhill.

This is a story as old as capitalism itself. But a golden rule that I live by is to never sacrifice the quality of your product in order to save money. Quality control is crucial, especially for small businesses. Your products are a reflection of you and your business's values. Don't sabotage your own image just to save a few bucks.

Dropshipping could be the key.

Last, but not least, consider drop shipping as an option. Dropshipping allows you to sell your products without actually having to store the inventory yourself. Instead, the manufacturer or a wholesaler would be responsible for packaging and shipping your invention to customers when they order it.

In the end, you don't have to worry about correcting the inventory, storing excess product, or fulfilling orders as they come in. It takes a lot of stress off of you and your team so that you can focus on marketing and selling your invention.

Knowing When It's Time to Expand

Your invention is finally finding the success you always knew it would, and now you're thinking about expanding your business. While this is a huge and monumental step for you and your team, it is important to plan for growth just as carefully and diligently as you did when first creating and selling your product. Most businesses take at least one year to make a decent profit, so you may not be ready to expand, even if you have more business than you think you can handle. But, if you're unsure what step to take next, then follow these checkpoints and see if you are ready to take your small production to the next level.

You have more business than your team can handle.

There is a big difference between keeping up with consumer demands and being completely overwhelmed by how much work there is to be done. While you may be busy with manufacturing and managing your inventory, the line of needing to grow vs. scaling back is crossed when you and your team cannot physically meet the demands of the customers.

Start by going over your numbers, the inventory you are selling every month, the last six months of sales and marketing data, upcoming initiatives from the marketing team, special events or holidays that are approaching, etc. Scaling up can be as comfortable as putting on the right sized pair of shoes, or it can put you out of business, adding costs to your budget that can't be met. Make sure that the boost in revenue isn't just a fluke, but the market's real thirst for your product.

You have a strong team that you can trust.

Look at the team you have now. Can you see yourself working with the same strong players in two, three, or five years from now? Are your staff members as invested in growing the business to the next level? If you answered 'no,' to any of these questions, then you are looking at the holes within your system.

The saying goes, "a team is only as strong as its weakest player," and it's true. Your staff is who carries the business and are trusted to give one hundred percent every time they clock in. If you can't trust the people on your team now, then it may be time to make some strategic hires, which can benefit you greatly in the future.

When I was managing a business a few years ago, I made the difficult decision of getting rid of a few people. In return, I found amazing employees who had better skillsets that helped solve issues within our branch of the business.

One of the new staff had great cleaning skills and was an expert with customer service. Another hire had a background in graphic design and contributed to storyboards for our advertisements. The end result was our branch doing better than any other location and our annual sales skyrocketing.

The point is, while it can be scary to fire someone or to invest in a new hire, you are doing yourself a favor in designing the team that will be carrying your business.

Even if you plan on selling your invention in the future, you need a strong foundation of people you can trust and rely on to get you to that point. Take this opportunity to create your dream team of employees, and watch your business soar.

You are running out of space.

This may seem like an obvious checkpoint, but it's important, nonetheless. When you literally have no more room for your inventory and not enough space for your staff to work, then it's time to expand into a space that has more square footage.

You are meeting your goals.

The best plans are the ones that have a roadmap to guide you, and within the roadmap should be milestones that measure your success. It's a standard to set goals within your business. But what happens when you've reached them all? Do you sell your business and move on? Or do you expand your company and work harder to grow?

If you have laid out your goals and general timeline of success, and have consistently met your milestones and been ahead of schedule for a while now, then it's time to expand. On the other hand, if you are constantly falling short and find it difficult to manage certain aspects of the business, then you may need to step back and reassess.

You have the funds to make it happen.

Now that you own a successful business, money isn't as tight as it was in the beginning. The best way to know whether or not you are ready to expand is by how much money you are making. Are you getting paid -not just your staff? Have you started a savings account, and has it been growing steadily over the last few months?

Even if your business is doing great on paper, you need to ensure that you have a positive cash flow before pursuing expansion. I know that there are dozens of options for small business and personal loans, but if your sales have been flat or you, as the owner, aren't getting paid, then it's not the time to expand. At least, not yet.

Selling Your Invention and Taking a Payoff

If your dream doesn't involve owning a business, or if you would rather be the creative mind behind inventions instead of the one selling it, then you might have the option of selling your idea to another company. This was a difficult decision for me when the time finally came to sell my idea.

I saw great success in creating, selling, and marketing my invention, but didn't enjoy the lifestyle that came with managing the business by myself. I'm more of the creative type anyway, and I saw the benefits that came with letting go of my idea. Even if you are really attached to your current invention, you always have the option of creating something new and selling that idea to a company. Which brings me to my first point.

How to Sell Your Idea to a Company

As an innovator, how to sell your ideas to a company is an important skill to know. And yes, it is a skill that can be learned, practiced, and mastered. You don't have to be the savviest businessman in the world to have a great idea for a product or enterprise. All you need is inspiration, creativity, and drive to make it happen. After the final product comes opportunity. You already know how to market your invention, but there are other options available -and you should be aware of them all.

Taking a Payoff

A payoff is the fastest method of selling your idea and getting paid for it. It allows the inventor to continue creating while getting money immediately following the finalization of their product. Taking a payoff is ideal for individuals who need fast money, want to start a retirement fund, or see their invention as a means to an end. However, it is absolutely crucial that any inventor who seeks to attain a payoff seal their ownership over any intellectual property. Otherwise, any potential purchasers will just steal the idea and create their own product.

If you are interested in pursuing this route, then you need to ensure that all bases are covered. That includes asking a suitable company to sign a nondisclosure settlement before pitching your invention. This can also contribute an additional benefit of strengthening your product's case and enhancing its sales value. You should also have a functioning prototype to display and include survey information and letters of intent from any potential shoppers, as these will both bolster your product's legitimacy.

You should beware of approaching too many firms in hopes of striking a deal. Consumers need exclusivity, and sharing your innovation with too many people can backfire. If you have a full-time position outside of your inventing, then you need to research your employee rights. An employer may potentially maintain the rights to an employee's invention if any work on the product is done within the enterprise during office hours.

This is exactly what happened with Tim Burton and his characters for The Nightmare Before Christmas. He drew his protagonist Jack Skellington and invented the concept for the movie while writing a poem when working for Disney, and part of his rights to the creative material was claimed by the mega-corporation. The lesson is to be careful about when you choose to work on your projects and with whom you share them with. You should also keep in mind that selling your idea for a payoff eliminates any claim or glory to the success of a product.

Taking a Percentage of Sales

If taking a fast payoff is not ideal, then you have another option in licensing your idea. For example, if an inventor has an idea that has a significant shelf life within the market, they can request a perpetual reduction of gross sales, rather than an outright single payment. When it comes to licensing an idea, the inventor will usually get a smaller preliminary cost between five and fifteen percent, taken from the individual sale of each unit. This might be a reasonable solution for cell phone app developers and other inventors within the tech space.

To ensure that the company or firm you partner with stays accountable for manufacturing and marketing the product, you can request a "finest efforts" clause in the licensing agreement. This will require the company to promote as much merchandise as possible and specify manufacturing, shipping, and gross sales goals. This will provide some security in the amount of money you make while licensing your idea.

Do You Want to Give the Idea Away?

Giving your idea away for free? Sounds a little insane, especially when you've put years into product development. But, this is actually a common practice -especially for individuals who care more about the concept than the money and want to help the world by using their passion.

Many professionals in the academic and health care fields choose to partner with an entrepreneur or enterprise and sign a settlement that allows that party to use the idea freely, but also with a clear purpose. Sometimes, it isn't about fame or money, it's just about creating and helping others.

If you have put all of your time, energy, and passion into this invention, then sometimes the best thing you can do is sit tight and wait until you feel fully ready to pursue a buyout or partnership. Oftentimes aspiring entrepreneurs and inventors sit on their ideas and visions because they don't feel ready.

Children, work, school, and other obligations will always contribute to a slow or reluctant start. But if you have a passion for an idea and feel strongly that it can make a difference, whether it's for a large group of people or just for your family, then you have a responsibility to yourself to see it through.

Conclusion

Thank you once again for taking the time to read my book. I hope that you feel inspired and more motivated than ever to get started on your invention and dive headfirst into the world of innovation and creativity.

I wrote this book because I had an important message to share. And that message is: it doesn't matter where you come from or what resources a person has available if they have the drive, work ethic, and passion for an idea, then they can be successful and see that idea become a reality. The success behind my invention may have had some luck, but I also worked tirelessly and relentlessly to manifest it. And I believe that you can do the same.

I wanted this book to be a useful and practical roadmap for anyone who seeks to create and build. I put all the knowledge and experience I have in these pages, and if it helps even just one person bring their invention to life, then it will have fulfilled its purpose.

I wish you nothing but the best on your journey to launch. I hope to see one of your creations in my own internet browsing and storefront shopping.

I sincerely hope this book has helped you in some way. If I have inspired you, please consider leaving a review where you purchased this book online. Reviews can help me to understand what you thought of the book and will help me to be able to be published more in the future. I would really appreciate it!

www.ingramcontent.com/pod-product-compliance
Lightning Source LLC
Chambersburg PA
CBHW071400210526
45465CB00001B/182